Perfect Behavior

Perfect Behavior

With pictures by RALPH BARTON

A guide for ladies and gentlemen in all Social Crises

Those who are not self-possessed obtrude and pain us.—EMERSON

Essex, Connecticut

Perfect Behavior

by DONALD OGDEN STEWART

A parody outline of etiquette by the Author of "A Parody Outline of History"

Introduction by JOSEPH EPSTEIN

The perfect gentleman is he who never unintentionally causes pain.—OLD PROVERB

An imprint of Globe Pequot, the trade division of
The Rowman & Littlefield Publishing Group, Inc.
4501 Forbes Blvd., Ste. 200
Lanham, MD 20706
www.rowman.com

Distributed by NATIONAL BOOK NETWORK

British Library Cataloguing in Publication Information available

Library of Congress Cataloging-in-Publication Data available

ISBN 9781493069248 (hardcover) | ISBN 9781493071395 (epub)

TO THE BRIDEGROOM WHOSE WEDDING WAS RUINED
BECAUSE THE BRIDE CAME DOWN THE AISLE
ON THE RIGHT INSTEAD OF THE LEFT
ARM OF HER FATHER

With Deepest Sympathy

Contents

[vii]

Perfect Behavior

Introduction

JOSEPH EPSTEIN

DONALD OGDEN STEWART was a member of the Algonquin Round Table, the group that, beginning in 1919 and ending in 1929, met for lunch at the Algonquin Hotel on 44th Street in New York and referred to itself as "the Vicious Circle." Among the group's best-known members were Dorothy Parker, George S. Kaufman, Robert Benchley, Harold Ross, Edna Ferber, Deems Taylor, and Franklin P. Adams. Unlike the great highbrow artists of the same period—James Joyce, Marcel Proust, Ezra Pound, T. S. Eliot—the members of the Round Table sought commercial success for their books, their plays on Broadway, and later for the films they wrote for Hollywood. Above all, they shared a sense of humor, one that, with the sword of wit, was dedicated to puncturing pretension.

[3]

Introduction

A few notable examples of Round Table wit: Dorothy Parker, having a door held open for her by Clare Boothe Luce who said "Age before Beauty," retorted, as she passed through the door, "Pearls before swine." When made pregnant by a well-known casanova of the day, Parker remarked, "That's what I get for putting all my eggs in one bastard." George S. Kaufman, famously neurotic though he was, explained his dropping out of psychotherapy because the therapist "asked too many personal questions." A noted philanderer, Kaufman told Irving Berlin that he would have liked Berlin's song "Always" better if it had been called "Thursdays."

Doubtless Donald Ogden Stewart (1894–1980) had a delicious *mot* or two of this sort to his credit—wit was after all the price of admission to the Algonquin Round Table—though none is recorded. Stewart was born in Columbus, Ohio, attended public school there and, later, Yale. He wrote plays and, in 1920, published *A Parody Outline of History*, satirizing H. G. Wells' *Outline of History*. In the 1920s Stewart went off to Hollywood and wrote, adapted, or

[4]

supplied additional dialogue for more than forty
films. For one of them, *The Philadelphia Story*
(1940), an adaptation of the Philip Barry play
of the same title, he won an Oscar for the best
screenplay.

Although he had earlier mocked Dorothy
Parker for her interest in the famous Sacco-Van-
zetti trial, Stewart himself became politicized
in the 1930s. In his excellent introduction to
Not Much Fun: The Lost Poems of Dorothy Parker,
Stuart Silverstein notes that Stewart "veered
hard to the left." After being divorced by his his
wife, Beatrice (one of Dorothy Parker's dearest
friends), "Stewart," Silverstein writes, "married
Leonore (Ella) Winter, the attractive Austra-
lia-born widow of the muckraker Lincoln Steffens. After the Cold War, a former Communist
apparatchik claimed that Ella had for several
years been 'one of the most trusted party agents
for the West Coast' when she met Stewart. She
was assigned to infiltrate Hollywood and to target people such as Stewart, as she had done
with Steffens." According to Silverstein, "Stewart was pleasant and sincere, but he was also a

political naïf who was easy prey for someone like Ella." He was blacklisted for his politics in 1950, and he and his wife left the country to live in England.

Donald Ogden Stewart is not remembered for his politics but for his light-hearted and high-spirited humor. In *Perfect Behavior, A Guide for Ladies and Gentlemen in All Social Crises*, he found a perfect subject for this humor. The book was published in 1922; the date is significant. The Volstead Act (1919–33), otherwise known as Prohibition, the law against the serving and drinking of all alcoholic beverages, was very much in force. In 1922, also, Emily Post's book *Etiquette* was atop all the bestseller lists in the country, and the phrase "according to Emily Post" came to stand for the last word on social conduct of every sort. If the larger theme of *Perfect Behavior* is the comic limitations of dispensing advice on everything from addressing letters to setting tables to conversation generally, the book's immediate target is *Etiquette*.

In the early decades of the twentieth century, social class loomed much larger than it does today. The arduous climb up the social ladder was a major preoccupation of Americans especially—witness its extensive role in the novels of among others Edith Wharton, Theodore Dreiser, and Sinclair Lewis. Mistaking the fish for the salad fork, lapsing into ungrammatical or even too colloquial or intimate speech, dressing wrongly for the dinner party, the opera, the weekend in the country, could stifle that climb at mid-rung. Status nervousness was endemic, getting the small things right, above all avoiding social mistakes, was felt to be crucial, which in good part explains the success of Emily Post's book.

I am not sure that I can myself tell the difference between a fish and salad fork, or if in past decades I have sat down to a meal in which both were in service. The only two bits of etiquette I myself consciously observe is at table never to pass dishes across my body and to congratulate a man but never a woman upon his or her recent engagement or marriage, for to congratulate a woman is to suggest that she has successfully caught, or entrapped, a man into marriage.

Introduction

We all have various bits of disregard for etiquette that offend us. In the seventeenth edition of *Etiquette*, published in 2004 and edited by Emily Post's granddaughter Peggy Post, Ms. Post bemoans the passing of the phrase "You're welcome" and its replacement by "No problem," "There's no need to thank me," or "It really wasn't anything." A bit of etiquette, or rather want of etiquette, that slightly yet genuinely offends me is being addressed in e-mail by a stranger as "Hi Joe."

Digital culture has brought out the need for new rules of etiquette. In the seventeenth edition of *Etiquette*, for example, there are no fewer than ten pages on the etiquette of e-mail, including the "Top Ten E-Mail Transgressions." Here those transgressions are:

1. Forwarding an off-color joke
2. Detailing a personal mishap
3. Writing a message in capital letters
4. Spreading gossip
5. Discussing personally sensitive issues
6. Criticizing another person

[8]

7. Complaining about work or one's boss
8. Using e-mail to dodge discussing diffi-cult-to-face issues
9. Going into detail about your own or another person's health problems
10. Arguing with family or friends

Follow this sensible advice and you are unlikely ever to commit an online faux pas—and quite as unlikely ever again to write an interesting e-mail.

Donald Ogden Stewart begins *Perfect Behavior* in straight-faced fashion, with a few words about love: "Courtship is one of the oldest of social customs, even antedating such long-es-tablished usages as marriage, or the wearing of white neckties with full evening dress." But things soon enough get goofily, wonderfully crazy, such as setting afire the house of a young woman one wishes to meet, then setting up "a few feet of stout manilla rope or clothes-line, from any of the better-class hardware stores" (note the details: "the stout manilla rope," "one of the better-class hardware stores"), which the

[9]

young woman is certain to trip over while fleeing her burning house. Stewart writes: "This is your opportunity to obtain an introduction. Stepping up to her and touching your hat politely, you say, in a well modulated voice, 'I beg your pardon, Miss Doe, but I cannot help noticing that you are lying prone on the sidewalk." Then, if she does not answer, you offer her your card and another of your cards for her mother. Stewart ends his paragraph: "Be sure that the cards are clean, as the name on the calling card is generally sufficient for identification purposes without the addition of the thumb-print."

Alcohol, make that boozing, places an extensive role in Donald Ogden Stewart's pages—the role, chiefly, of destroyer of etiquette and of decorum generally. At a Halloween party in *Perfect Behavior*, twelve quarts of gin replace water in the bobbing for apples tub, and "the effect on the bobbers was of course extremely comical, except for the unfortunate conduct of two gentlemen, one of whom went to sleep in the tub, the other going so far as to throw all the floating fruit at the hostess' pet Pomeranian."

[10]

Joseph Epstein

"'Drinking' has of course always been a popular sport among the members of the better classes of society," Stewart writes, "but never has the enthusiasm for this pastime been so great in America as since the advent of 'prohibition.'" Stewart devotes a short chapter to "Etiquette for Dry Agents," those people paid to enforce the Volstead Act in both public and private places. "And if Mr. Volstead has a dress suit," Stewart writes, "you might take him with you, and show him how beautifully Prohibition is working and how enthusiastic the better classes of American society are about it," which of course they weren't. Underlining the essential hypocrisy behind Prohibition, Stewart supplies a letter from a Congressman ordering his own liquor: "Tell that fellow on Mulberry Street that I will pay $135 for a case of Scotch and $90 for gin delivered and not a cent more."

Amusing touches play throughout *Perfect Behavior*. Stewart advises that a young gentleman, when first calling upon a young woman, should plan his conversation well in advance:

Introduction

"Select some topic in which your lady friend will be interested, such as, for example, the removal of adenoids and tonsils." He goes on to cite statistics on adenoid and tonsil removal and suggests searching *Bartlett's Familiar Quotations* for apt verses dealing with throat troubles.

The obvious in Stewart is played for small but genuine laughs. "Each time you will be handed another drink," he writes, "which you may take in either your right or left hand." After finishing packing a suitcase for a trip, "you can immediately unstrap and unlock it in order to put in the tooth paste and shaving brush which you forgot to bring from the bathroom." In a passage about "the etiquette of changing a tire," you will leave the scene of the change "as well as [your] father's best 'jack' and set of tire tools." Bridal showers "should be informal and only her [the bride's] dearest or wealthiest friends should be invited."

Two odd references to *The Atlantic Monthly* pop up in *Perfect Behavior*. In one, back issues of the magazine are suggested as a proper gift for a bridal shower. In the other, young girls are advised that "the surest way to protect yourself from any unwelcome advances is to buy a copy of the *Atlantic Monthly* and carry it, in plain view." Did Stewart have a grudge against the magazine and its editors, featuring it as he does here as a badge of dullness? Alas, we shall probably never know.

In the chapter on the etiquette of correspondence and invitations, there is a letter from the mother of a president of the United States advising him, in motherishly nagging fashion, to be sure to remember to wear his long underwear in winter, not to forget to see his dentist, and noting that she saw "a picture of you at the 'movies' the other evening and you were making a speech in the rain with a hat or rubbers." This letter reminded me of the old joke about the first Jewish president of the United States who calls his mother to make sure she will attend the first Passover seder ever to be held in the White House, only to be turned down because his mother has already accepted an invitation to the seder given by "your brother, the doctor."

[13]

Introduction

The chapter devoted to concert- and opera-going is chiefly about one-upmanship. Here the advice is never to show any enthusiasm for music composed after 1870. At the opera the reader is told to remark that "you don't really care for the human voice." Instruction in shushing anyone making noise at a musical performance advises: "Should he continue the offense, a severe frown must accompany the next 'sh-sh,' a lorgnette—if available—aiding greatly to the rebuke."

Sometimes the letters quoted in *Perfect Behavior* suggest a touch of sadness. One is from a male fiancé who is an information bore, who cannot stop blithering on even in a letter. Another is from a digressive old man writing a letter to an editor that is filled with Latin tags and hopeless reminiscence. Yet another is from a young girl off at boarding school who attempts to discourage her parents from visiting her there because she is clearly ashamed of them, and especially of her father: "And please, mother dear, make him put those 'stogies' of his in an inside pocket and do you mind, mother, not wearing that brooch father's employees gave you last Christmas?"

Joseph Epstein

Perfect Behavior is not merely a superior parody of Emily Post's *Etiquette* but a book about the comedy of life, its pretensions, contradictions, injustices, struggles for dignity, and endless amusements.

PERFECT BEHAVIOR

CHAPTER ONE: The Etiquette of Courtship

A FEW WORDS ABOUT LOVE

COURTSHIP is one of the oldest of social customs, even antedating in some countries such long-established usages as marriage, or the wearing of white neckties with full evening dress. The beginnings of the etiquette of courtship were apparently connected in some way with the custom of "love" between the sexes, and many of the old amatory forms still survive in the modern courtship. It is generally agreed among students of the history of etiquette that when "love" first began to become popular among the better class of younger people they took to it with such avidity that it was necessary to devise some sort of rules for the conduct of formal or informal love-making. These rules, together with various amendments, now constitute the etiquette of courtship.

Suppose, for example, that you are a young gentleman named Richard Roe desirous of entering upon a formal courtship with some refined young girl of fashion. You are also, being a college graduate, engaged in the bond business. One morning there comes into your financial institution a young lady, named Dorothy Doe, who at once attracts your attention by her genteel manners, as exemplified by the fact that she calls the president of your company "father." So many young people seem to think it "smart" to refer to their parents as "dad" or "my old man"; you are certain, as soon as you hear her say "Hello, father" to your employer, that she is undoubtedly a worthy object of courtship.

CORRECT INTRODUCTIONS; HOW TO MAKE THEM

YOUR first step should be, of course, the securing of an introduction. Introductions still play an important part in social intercourse, and many errors are often perpetrated by those ignorant of *savoir faire* (correct form). When introducing a young lady to a stranger for example, it is not *au fait* (correct form) to simply say, "Mr. Roe, I want you to shake hands with my friend Dorothy." Under the rules of the *beau monde* (correct form) this would probably be done as follows: "Dorothy (or Miss Doe), shake hands with Mr. Roe." Always give the name of the lady first, unless you are introducing some one to the President of the United States, the Archbishop of Canterbury, a member of the nobility above a baron, or a customer. The person who is being "introduced" then extends his (or her) right ungloved hand and says, "Shake." You "shake," saying at the same time, "It's warm (cool) for November (May)," to which the other replies, "I'll say it is."

This brings up the interesting question of introducing two people to each other, neither of whose names you can remember. This is generally done by saying very quickly to one

[19]

of the parties, "Of course you know Miss Unkunkunk." Say the last "unk" very quickly, so that it sounds like any name from Ab to Zinc. You might even sneeze violently. Of course, in nine cases out of ten, one of the two people will at once say, "I didn't get the name," at which you laugh, "Ha! Ha! Ha!" in a carefree manner several times, saying at the same time, "Well, well—so you didn't get the name—you didn't get the name —well, well." If the man still persists in wishing to know who it is to whom he is being introduced, the best procedure consists in simply braining him on the spot with a club or convenient slab of paving stone.

The "introduction," in cases where you have no mutual friend to do the introducing, is somewhat more difficult but can generally be arranged as follows:

Procure a few feet of stout manila rope or clothes-line, from any of the better-class hardware stores. Ascertain (from the Social Register, preferably) the location of the young lady's residence, and go there on some dark evening about nine o'clock. Fasten the rope across the sidewalk in front of the residence about six inches or a foot from the ground. Then, with the aid of a match and some kerosene, set fire to the young lady's house in several places and retire behind a convenient tree. After some time, if she is at home, she will probably be forced to run out of her house to avoid being burned to death. In her excitement she will fail to notice the rope which you have stretched across the sidewalk and will fall. This is your opportunity to obtain an introduction. Stepping up to her and touching your hat politely, you say, in a well-modulated voice, "I beg your pardon, Miss Doe, but I cannot help noticing that you are lying prone on the sidewalk." If she is well-bred, she will not at first speak to you, as you are a perfect stranger. This silence, however, should be your cue to once more tip your hat and remark, "I realize, Miss Doe, that I have not had the honor of an introduction, but you will admit that you are lying prone on the sidewalk. Here is my card—and here is one

[21]

Perfect Behavior

for Mrs. Doe, your mother." At that you should hand her two plain engraved calling cards, each containing your name and address. If there are any other ladies in her family—aunts, grandmothers, et cetera—it is correct to leave cards for them also. Be sure that the cards are clean, as the name on the calling card is generally sufficient for identification purposes without the addition of the thumb-print.

When she has accepted your cards, she will give you one of hers, after which it will be perfectly correct for you to assist her to rise from the sidewalk. Do not, however, press your attentions further upon her at this time, but after expressing the proper regret over her misfortune it would be well to bow and retire.

CARDS AND FLOWERS

THE next day, however, you should send flowers, enclosing another of your cards. It might be well to write some message on the card recalling the events of the preceding

[22]

Every one knows that table manners betray one's bringing-up mercilessly. The young man in the picture has good reason to wish a meteorite would fall on him. His perpendicularity has just been restored by a deft upward movement of Aunt Harriet's shoulder, upon which he had inadvertently rested his head during a quiet snooze while Cousin Edna was making her little speech at the Bridal Dinner. PERFECT BEHAVIOR *would have Pasteurized him against even Bridal Dinners.*

When a woman recognizes and nods to a man to whom she has been formally introduced several times, or to whom she has been married, is the man expected to accept the greeting and politely lift his hat or should he lift both his hat and his toupee? Street etiquette is disposed of, authoritatively and finally in PERFECT BEHAVIOR.

You are, let us pretend, walking in the park. You come upon two benches arranged as shown in the above diagram. Would you know which bench it would be proper to sit on if you are (1) a young man just out of college—(2) a rather homely young woman? To avoid embarrassment look this up in PERFECT BEHAVIOR.

A jolly crowd is boarding the 4:56 for a house-party in the suburbs. The gentleman at the right, having been educated abroad, has never learned to play the ukelele, the banjo, the jew's harp or the saxophone, and is, with the best intentions in the world, attempting to contribute his share to the gaiety of the coming evenings by bringing along his player-piano. Would you—be honest!—have recognized his action as a serious social blunder without having referred to PERFECT BEHAVIOR?

The young mother in the picture is traveling from
one point to another in a Pullman. In the effort
to commit as great a nuisance as possible, she has
provided her child with a banana and a hard boiled
egg. Not having dipped into the chapter on travel
in PERFECT BEHAVIOR, she is ignorant of the fact
that a peach would have produced quite as much
mess and far more permanent stains and a folding
cup for the water cooler would have spread the
disturbance over a wider area.

evening—nothing intimate, but simply a reminder of your first meeting and a suggestion
that you might possibly desire to continue the
acquaintanceship. Quotations from poetry of
the better sort are always appropriate; thus,
on this occasion, it might be nice to write on
the card accompanying the flowers—" 'This is
the forest primeval'—H. W. Longfellow," or
" 'Take, oh take, those lips away'—W. Shakespeare." You will find there are hundreds
of lines equally appropriate for this and other
occasions, and in this connection it might be
well to display a little originality at times by
substituting pertinent verses of your own in
place of the conventional quotations. For
example—"This is the forest primeval, I
regret your last evening's upheaval," shows
the young lady in question that not only are
you well-read in classic poetry, but also you
have no mean talent of your own. Too much
originality, however, is dangerous, especially
in polite social intercourse, and I need hardly
remind you that the floors of the social ocean

are watered with the tears of those who seek to walk on their own hook.

Within a week after you have sent the young lady the flowers, you should receive a polite note of thanks, somewhat as follows: "My dear Mr. Roe: Those lovely flowers came quite as a surprise. They are lovely, and I cannot thank you enough for your thoughtfulness. Their lovely fragrance fills my room as I write, and I wish to thank you again. It was lovely of you."

FLOWERS AND THEIR MESSAGE IN COURTSHIP

IT is now time to settle down to the more serious business of courtship. Her letter shows beyond the shadow of a figurative doubt that she is "interested," and the next move is "up to you." Probably she will soon come into the office to see her father, in which case you should have ready at hand some appropriate gift, such as, for example, a nice potted geranium. Great care should be taken, however, that it is a plant of the correct species, for in the etiquette of courtship all flowers have different meanings and many a promising affair has been ruined because a suitor sent his lady a buttercup, meaning "That's the last dance I'll ever take you to, you big cow," instead of a plant with a more tender significance. Some of the commoner flowers and their meaning in courtship are as follows:

Fringed Gentian—"I am going out to get a shave. Back at 3:30."

Poppy—"I would be proud to be the father of your children."

Golden-rod—"I hear that you have hay-fever."

Tuberose—"Meet me Saturday at the Fourteenth Street subway station."

Blood-root—"Aunt Kitty murdered Uncle Fred Thursday."

Dutchman's Breeches—"That case of Holland gin and Old Tailor has arrived. Come on over."

Iris—"Could you learn to love an optician?"

Perfect Behavior

Aster—"Who was that stout Jewish-looking party I saw you with in the hotel lobby Friday?"

Deadly Nightshade — "Pull down those blinds, quick!"

Passion Flower—"Phone Main 1249—ask for Eddie."

Raspberry—"I am announcing my engagebent to Charlie O'Keefe Tuesday."

Wild Thyme—"I have seats for the Hippodrome Saturday afternoon."

The above flowers can also be combined to make different meanings, as, for example, a bouquet composed of three tuberoses and some Virginia creeper generally signifies the following, "The reason I didn't call for you yesterday was that I had three inner tube punctures, besides a lot of engine trouble in that old car I bought in Virginia last year. Gosh, I'm sorry!"

But to return to the etiquette of our present courtship. As Miss Doe leaves the office you follow her, holding the potted plant in your left hand. After she has gone a few paces you step up to her, remove your hat (or cap) with your right hand, and offer her the geranium, remarking, "I beg your pardon, miss, but didn't you drop this?" A great deal depends upon the manner in which you offer the plant and the way she receives it. If you hand it to her with the flower pointing upward it means, "Dare I hope?" Reversed, it signifies, "Your petticoat shows about an inch, or an inch and a half." If she receives the plant in her right hand, it means, "I am"; left hand, "You are"; both hands—"He, she or it is." If, however, she takes the pot firmly in both hands and breaks it with great force on your head, the meaning is usually negative and your only correct course of procedure is a hasty bow and a brief apology.

RECEIVING AN INVITATION TO CALL

LET us suppose, however, that she accepts the geranium in such a manner that you are encouraged to continue the acquaintance. Your next move should be a request for an

Perfect Behavior

invitation to call upon her at her home. This should, above all things, not be done crudely. It is better merely to suggest your wish by some indirect method such as, "Oh—so you live on William Street. Well, well! I often walk on William Street in the evening, but I have never called on any girl there—*yet.*" The "yet" may be accompanied by a slight raising of your eyebrows, a wink, or a friendly nudge with your elbow. Unless she is unusually "dense" she will probably "take the hint" and invite you to come and see her some evening. At once you should say, *"What* evening? How about *to-night?"* If she says that she is already engaged for that evening, take a calendar out of your pocket and remark, "Tomorrow? Wednesday? Thursday? Friday? I really have no engagements between now and October. Saturday? Sunday?" This will show her that you are really desirous of calling upon her and she will probably say, "Well, I think I am free Thursday night, but you had better telephone me first."

The Etiquette of Courtship

ON Thursday morning, therefore, you should go to a public telephone-booth in order to call the young lady's house. The etiquette of telephoning is quite important and many otherwise perfectly well-bred people often make themselves conspicuous because they do not know the correct procedure in using this modern but almost indispensable invention. Upon entering the telephone-booth, which is located, say, in some drug store, you remove the receiver from the hook and deposit the requisite coin in the coin box. After an interval of some minutes a young lady (referred to as "Central") will ask for your "Number, please." Suppose, for example, that you wish to get Bryant 4310. Remove your hat politely and speak that number into the mouthpiece. "Central" will then say, "Rhinelander 4310." To which you reply, *"No,* Central—*Bryant* 4310." Central then says, "I beg your pardon—Bryant 4310," to which you reply, "Yes, please." In a few min-

[29]

utes a voice at the other end of the line says, "Hello," to which you answer, "Is Miss Doe at home?" The voice then says, "Who?" You say, "Miss Doe, please—Miss Dorothy Doe." You then hear the following, "Wait a minute. Say, Charlie, is they anybody works around here by the name of Doe? There's a guy wants to talk to a Miss Doe. Here—you answer it." Another voice then says, "Hello." You reply "Hello." He says, "What do you want?" You reply, "I wish to speak to Miss Dorothy Doe." He says, "What department does she work in?" You reply, "Is this the residence of J. Franklin Doe, President of the First National Bank?" He says, "Wait a minute." You wait a minute. You wait several. Another voice—a new voice says— "Hello." You reply "Hello." He says, "Give me Stuyvesant 8864." You say, "But I'm trying to get Miss Doe—Miss Dorothy Doe." He says, "Who?" You say, "Is this the residence of —" He says, "Naw—this is Goebel Brothers, Wholesale Grocers—what number do you want?" You say, "Bryant

Not realizing his mistake, the Groom stands waiting for the Bridal Procession, apparently in high spirits and the best of health. Such an attitude toward a wedding is in the worst possible taste. PERFECT BEHAVIOR *tells all about the correct appearance and conduct of Bridegrooms.*

The Best Man has just been introduced to the Maid of Honor. Instead of waiting for her to extend her hand and make the acknowledgment, he has turned on his heel and bolted from the room. This constitutes a social blunder, after the commission of which he could never again, in polite society, be considered quite a gentleman. PERFECT BEHAVIOR would have told him how the man of birth and breeding learns to face anything with perfect "Sang froid."

The Groom has just presented his Best Man to
his sister, who, though she is more than eager
to make every one feel at home, has failed to make
at once the pun "de rigueur" on the words "best
man." An awkward silence has ensued. What
is to be done? Should one of the gentlemen fill
the breach by making the pun for her? If so,
which? PERFECT BEHAVIOR covers the whole
subject of making the "best man" pun authoritatively.

The young man at the right does not know how to drink. Nevertheless, he has been selected by a friend to act as Best Man at his wedding and has attended the Bachelor Dinner. Instead of doing what he should do under the circumstances, he is making himself conspicuous by remaining coherent while the others sing "Mademoiselle from Alabam'." Had the Bridegroom provided himself with a copy of PERFECT BEHAVIOR he would have known better than to have selected him

4310." He says, "Well, this is Rhinelander 4310." You then hang up the receiver and count twenty. The telephone bell then rings, and inasmuch as you are the only person near the phone you take up the receiver and say, "Hello." A female voice, says, "Hello, dearie—don't you know who this is?" You say, politely but firmly, "No." She says, "Guess!" You guess "Mrs. Warren G. Harding." She says, "No. This is Ethel. Is Walter there?" You reply, "Walter?" She says, "Ask him to come to the phone, will you? He lives up-stairs over the drug store. Just yell 'Walter' at the third door down the hall. Tell him Ethel wants to speak to him—no, wait—tell him it's Madge." Being a gentleman, you comply with the lady's request. After bringing Walter to the phone, you obligingly wait for some twenty minutes while he converses with Ethel—no, Madge. When he has finished, you once more enter the booth and tell "Central" you want Bryant 4310. After a few minutes "Central" says, "What number did you call?" You say patiently, "Bryant 4310."

[31]

She replies, "Bryant 4310 has been changed to
Schuyler 6372." You ask for Schuyler 6372.
Finally a woman's voice says, "Yass." You
say, "Is Miss Doe in?" She replies, "Yass."
You say, "May I speak to her?" She says,
"Who?" You reply, "You said Miss Doe was
at home, didn't you?" She replies, "Yass."
You say, "Well, may I speak to her?" The
voice says, "Who?" You shout, "Miss Doe."
The voice says, "She ban out." You shriek,
"Oh, go to hell!" and assuming a graceful, easy
position in the booth, you proceed to tear the
telephone from the wall. Later on in the day,
when you have two or three hours of spare
time, you can telephone Miss Doe again and
arrange for the evening's visit.

MAKING THE FIRST CALL

THE custom of social "calls" between
young men and young women is one of
the prettiest of etiquette's older conventions,
and one around which clusters a romantic
group of delightful traditions. In this day
and generation, what with horseless carriages,

electric telephones and telegraphs, and dirigible gas bags, a great many of the older forms have been allowed to die out, greatly, I believe, to our discredit. "Speed, not manners," seems to be the motto of this century. I hope that there still exist a few young men who care enough about "good form" to study carefully to perfect themselves in the art of "calling." Come, Tom, Dick and Harry—drop your bicycles for an afternoon and fill your minds with something besides steam engines and pneumatic tires!

The first call at the home of any young lady of fashion is an extremely important social function, and too great care can not be taken that you prepare yourself thoroughly in advance. It would be well to leave your work an hour or two earlier in the afternoon, so that you can go home and practice such necessary things as entering or leaving a room correctly. Most young men are extremely careless in this particular, and unless you rehearse yourself thoroughly in the proper procedure you are apt to find later on to your dismay that

[33]

you have made your exit through a window onto the fire-escape instead of through the proper door.

CONVERSATION AND SOME OF ITS USES

YOUR conversation should also be planned more or less in advance. Select some topic in which you think your lady friend will be interested, such as, for example, the removal of tonsils and adenoids, and "read up" on the subject so that you can discuss it in an intelligent manner. Find out, for example, how many people had tonsils removed in February, March, April. Contrast this with the same figures for 1880, 1890, 1900. Learn two or three amusing anecdotes about adenoids. Consult Bartlett's "Familiar Quotations" for appropriate verses dealing with tonsils and throat troubles. Finally, and above all, take time to glance through four or five volumes of Dr. Eliot's Five Foot Shelf, for nothing so completely marks the cultivated man as the ability to refer familiarly to the various volumes of the Harvard classics.

[34]

The Etiquette of Courtship

PROMPTLY at the time appointed you should arrive at the house where the young lady is staying. In answer to your ring a German police dog will begin to bark furiously inside the house, and a maid will finally come to the door. Removing your hat and one glove, you say, "Is Miss Doe home?" The maid replies, "Yass, ay tank so." You give her your card and the dog rushes out and bites you on either the right or left leg. You are then ushered into a room in which is seated an old man with a long white beard. He is fast asleep. "Dot's grampaw," says the maid, to which you reply, "Oh." She retires, leaving you alone with grampaw. After a while he opens his eyes and stares at you for a few minutes. He then says, "Did the dog bite you?" You answer, "Yes, sir." Grampaw then says, "He bites everybody," and goes back to sleep. Reassured, you light a cigaret. A little boy and girl then come to the door, and, after examining you carefully for sev-

[35]

eral minutes, they burst into giggling laughter and run away. You feel to see if you have forgotten to put on a necktie. A severe looking old lady then enters the room. You rise and bow. "I am Miss Doe's grandmother. Some one has been smoking in here," she says, and sits down opposite you. Her remark is not, however, a hint for a cigaret and you should not make the mistake of saying, "I've only got Fatimas, but if you care to try one—" It should be your aim to seek to impress yourself favorably upon every member of the young lady's family. Try to engage the grandmother in conversation, taking care to select subjects in which you feel she would be interested. Conversation is largely the art of "playing up" to the other person's favorite subject. In this particular case, for example, it would be a mistake to say to Miss Doe's grandmother, "Have you ever tried making synthetic gin?" or "Do you think any one will *ever* lick Dempsey?" A more experienced person, and some one who had studied the hobbies of old people, would probably begin by remarking,

[36]

The Etiquette of Courtship

"Well, I see that Jeremiah Smith died of cancer Thursday," or "That was a lovely burial they gave Mrs. Watts, wasn't it?" If you are tactful, you should soon win the old lady's favor completely, so that before long she will tell you all about her rheumatism and what grampaw can and can't eat.

Finally Miss Doe arrives. Her first words are, "Have you been waiting long? Hilda didn't tell me you were here," to which you reply, "No—I just arrived." She then says, "Shall we go in the drawing-room?" The answer to this is, "For God's sake, yes!" In a few minutes you find yourself alone in the drawing-room with the lady of your choice and the courtship proper can then begin.

The best way to proceed is gradually to bring the conversation around to the subject of the "modern girl." After your preliminary remarks about tonsils and adenoids have been thoroughly exhausted, you should suddenly say, "Well, I don't think girls—nice girls—are really that way." She replies, of course, *"What* way?" You answer, "Oh, the way they

[37]

are in these modern novels. This 'petting,' for instance." She says, *"What* 'petting'?" You walk over and sit down on the sofa beside her. "Oh," you say, "these novelists make me sick—they seem to think that in our generation every time a young man and woman are left alone on a lounge together, they haven't a thing better to do than put out the light and 'pet.' It's disgusting, isn't it?" "Isn't it?" she agrees and reaching over she accidentally pulls the lamp cord, which puts out the light.

On your first visit you should not stay after 12:30.

THE PROPOSAL PROPER

ABOUT the second or third month of a formal courtship it is customary for the man to propose matrimony, and if the girl has been "out" for three or four years and has several younger sisters coming along, it is customary for her to accept him. They then become "engaged," and the courtship is concluded.

Chapter Two

THE ETIQUETTE
OF ENGAGEMENTS
AND WEDDINGS

CHAPTER TWO: The Etiquette of Engagements and Weddings

THE HISTORIC ASPECT

"MATRIMONY," sings Homer, the poet, "is a holy estate and not lightly to be entered into." The "old Roman" is right. A modern wedding is one of the most intricate and exhausting of social customs. Young men and women of our better classes are now forced to devote a large part of their lives to acting as brides, grooms, ushers and bridesmaids at various elaborate nuptials. Weeks are generally required in preparation for an up-to-date wedding; months are necessary in recovering from such an affair. Indeed, some of the participants, notably the bride and groom, never quite get over the effects of a marriage.

It was not "always thus." Time was when the wedding was a comparatively simple affair. In the Paleolithic Age, for example, (as Mr. H. G. Wells of England points out in his able "Outline of History"), there is no evidence of any particular ceremony conjunctive with the marriage of "a male and a female." Even with the advent of Neolithic man, a wedding seems to have been consummated by the rather simple process of having the bridegroom crack the bride over the head with a plain, unornamented stone ax. There were no ushers—no bridesmaids. But shortly after that (c. 10,329—30 B.C. to be exact) two young Neoliths named Haig, living in what is now supposed to be Scotland, discovered that the prolonged distillation of common barley resulted in the creation of an amber-colored liquid which, when taken internally, produced a curious and not unpleasant effect.

This discovery had—and still has—a remarkable effect upon the celebration of the marriage rite. Gradually there grew up around the wedding a number of customs. With the Haig brothers' discovery of Scotch whiskey began, as a matter of course, the in-

stitution of the "bachelor dinner." "Neces-
sity is the mother of invention," and exactly
twelve years after the first "bachelor dinner"
came the discovery of bicarbonate of soda.
From that time down to the present day the
history of the etiquette of weddings has been
that of an increasing number of intricate forms
and ceremonies, each age having added its
particular bit of ritual. The modern wedding may be said to be, therefore, almost an
"Outline of History" itself.

ANNOUNCING THE ENGAGEMENT

LET us begin, first of all, with the duties of
one of the minor characters at a wedding
—the Groom. Suppose that you are an eligible young man named Richard Roe, who has
just become "engaged" to a young lady named
Dorothy Doe. If you really intend to "marry
the girl," it is customary that some formal announcement of the engagement be made, for
which you must have the permission of Miss
Dorothy and her father. It is not generally
difficult to become engaged to most girls, but

[43]

it will surprise you to discover how hard it is to get the young lady whom you believe to be your fiancée to consent to a public announcement of the fact. The reason for this probably is that an engagement which has been "announced" often leads to matrimony, and matrimony, in polite society, often lasts for several years.

After you have secured the girl's permission, it is next necessary that you notify her father of the engagement. In this particular case, as he happens to be your employer, the notification can take place in his office. First of all, however, it would be advisable to prepare some sort of speech in advance. Aim to put him as far as possible at his ease, lead up to the subject gradually and tactfully. Abruptness is never "good form." The following is suggested as a possible model.

"Good morning, Mr. Doe, say, I heard a good story from a traveling salesman last night. It seems that there was a young married couple—(here insert a good story about a young married couple). Wasn't that *rich?*

Yes, sir, marriage is a great thing—a great institution. Every young man ought to get married, don't you think? You do? Well, Mr. Doe, I've got a surprise for you, (here move toward the door). I'm going to (here open the door) marry (step out of the room) your daughter" (close the door quickly).

THE BRIDE-TO-BE

B EFORE the public announcement of the engagement it is customary for the bride-to-be to write personal letters to all other young men to whom she happens to be engaged at the time. These notes should be kindly, sympathetic and tactful. The same note can be written to all, provided there is no chance of their comparing notes. The following is suggested:

"Dear Bob—

Bob, I want you to be the very first to know that I am engaged to Richard Roe. I want you to like him, Bob, because he is a fine fellow and I would rather have you like him than

[45]

any one I know. I feel that he and I shall be very happy together, and I want you to be the first to know about it. Your friendship will always remain one of the brightest things in my life, Bob, but, of course, I probably won't be able to go to the Aiken dance with you now. Please don't tell anybody about it yet. I shall never forget the happy times you and I had together, Bob, and will you please return those silly letters of mine. I am sending you yours."

THE ENGAGEMENT LUNCHEON

THE engagement is generally announced at a luncheon given by the parents of the prospective bride. This is usually a small affair, only fifteen or twenty of the most intimate friends of the engaged "couple" being invited. It is one of the customs of engagement luncheons that all the guests shall be tremendously surprised at the news, and great care should be taken to aid them in carrying out this tradition. On the invitations, for example, should be written some misleading

[46]

Nothing so completely betrays the "Cockney" as a faulty knowledge of sporting terms. The young lady at the left has just returned from the hunting field hand-in-hand with the dashing "lead," who happens to be an eligible billionaire. Her hostess, the mother of the sub-deb at the right, has greeted her by hissing, "S—o—o! I see you've had a good day's hunting!" The use of this unsportsmanlike expression—instead of the correct "Hope you had a good run," or "Where did you find?"—at once discloses the hostess's mean origin and the young lady will almost certainly never accept another invitation to her house

In this work-a-day world, one is likely to forget that there is an etiquette of pleasure just as there is an etiquette of dancing or the opera. One often hears a charming hostess refuse to invite this or that person to her home for a game of billiards on the ground that he or she is a "bum sport" or a "rotten loser." The above scene illustrates one of the little, but conspicuous, blunders that people make. The gentleman, having missed his fifth consecutive shot, has broken his cue over his knee and is ripping the baize off the table with the sharp end. This display is not in the best taste.

Good form at the beach is still a question of debate. Some authorities on the subject insist that the Rubenesque type is preferable, while others claim that the Byzantine is more fashionable. One thing is certain—it is absolutely incorrect for ladies who weigh less than 75 or more than 275 pounds (avoir-dupois) to appear in costumes that would offend against modesty. It is also considered rude to hold one's swimming partner under water for more than the formal quarter of an hour.

phrase, such as "To meet General Pershing" or "Not to Announce the Engagement of our Daughter."

The announcement itself which should be made soon after the guests are seated, offers a splendid opportunity for the display of originality and should aim to afford the guest a surprise and perhaps a laugh, for laughter of a certain quiet kind is often welcome at social functions. One of the most favored methods of announcing an engagement is by the use of symbolic figures embodying the names of the affianced pair. Thus, for example, in the case of the present engagement of Richard Roe to Dorothy Doe it would be "unique" to have the first course at luncheon consist of a diminutive candy or paper-mâché doe seated amorously upon a heart shaped order of a shad roe. The guests will at first be mystified, but soon cries of "Oh, how sweet!" will arise and congratulations are then in order. Great care should be taken, however, that the symbolic figures are not misunderstood; it would be extremely embarrassing, for example, if in the

[47]

above instance, a young man named "Shad" or "Aquarium" were to receive the congratulations instead of the proper person.

Other suggestions for symbolistic announcements of some of the more common names are as follows:

"Cohan-O'Brien"—ice cream cones on a plate of O'Brien potatoes.

"Ames-Green—green ice cream in the shape of a man aiming at something.

"Thorne-Hoyt—figure of a man from Brooklyn pulling a thorn from foot with expression on his face signifying "This hoits."

"Bullitt-Bartlett—bartlett pears full of small 22 or 33 calibre bullets.

"Tweed-Ellis"—frosted cake in the shape of Ellis Island with a solitary figure of a man in a nice fitting tweed suit.

"Gordon-Fuller"—two paper-mâché figures —one representing a young man full of Gordon gin, the other representing a young man fuller.

"Hatch-Gillette"—figure of a chicken surprised at having hatched a safety razor.

[48]

"*Graves-Colgate*"—figure of a man brushing his teeth in a cemetery.

"*Heinz-Fish*"—57 assorted small fish tastily arranged on one plate.

SELECTING THE BRIDAL PARTY

A S soon as the engagement has been announced it is the duty of the prospective bride to select a maid-of-honor and eight or ten bridesmaids, while the groom must choose his best man and ushers. In making these selections it should be carefully borne in mind that no wedding party is complete without the following:

1 bridesmaid who danced twice with the Prince of Wales.

2 Bridesmaids who never danced more than once with anybody.

1 bridesmaid who doesn't "pet."

1 bridesmaid who was expelled from Miss Spence's.

1 bridesmaid who talks "Southern."

1 bridesmaid who met Douglas Fairbanks once.

1 bridesmaid who rowed on the crew at Wellesley.

1 usher who doesn't drink anything.

9 ushers who drink anything.

In some localities, following the announcement, it is customary for the bride's friends

[49]

to give for her a number of "showers." These are for the purpose of providing her with various necessities for her wedded household life. These affairs should be informal and only her dearest or wealthiest friends should be invited. A clever bride will generally arrange secretly for several of these "showers" by promising a certain percentage (usually 15% of the gross up to $500.00 and 25% bonus on all over that amount) to the friend who gives the party. Some of the more customary "showers" of common household articles for the new bride are toothpaste, milk of magnesia, screen doors, copies of Service's poems, Cape Cod lighters, pictures of "Age of Innocence" and back numbers of the "Atlantic Monthly."

INVITATIONS AND WEDDING PRESENTS

THE proper time to send out invitations to a wedding is between two and three weeks before the day set for the ceremony, although the out-of-town invitations should be mailed in plenty of time to allow the recipient to purchase and forward a suitable present.

As the gifts are received, a check mark should be placed after the name of the donor, together with a short description of the present and an estimate as to its probable cost. This list is to be used later, at the wedding reception, in determining the manner in which the bride is to greet the various guests. It has been found helpful by many brides to devise some sort of memory system whereby certain names immediately suggest certain responses, thus:

"Mr. Snodgrass—copy of "Highways and Byways in Old France"—c. $6.50—"how do you do, Mr. Snodgrass, have you met my mother?"

"Mr. Brackett—Solid silver candlesticks—$68.50"—"hello, Bob, you old peach. How about a kiss?"

The real festivities of a wedding start about three days before the ceremony, with the arrival of the "wedding party," in which party the most responsible position is that of best man. Let us suppose that you are to be the best man at the Roe-Doe nuptials. What are your duties?

[51]

In the first place, you must prepare your-self for the wedding by a course of training extending for over a month or more prior to the actual event. It should be your aim to work yourself into such a condition that you can go for three nights without sleep, talk for hours to the most impossibly stupid of young women, and consume an unending amount of alcohol. You are then prepared for the bachelor dinner, the bridal dinner, the brides-maids, the wedding, and the wedding recep-tion.

DUTIES OF THE BEST MAN

UPON your arrival in the city where the wedding is to take place you will be met by the bridegroom, who will take you to the home of the bride where you are to stay. There you are met by the bride's father. "This is my best man," says the groom. "The best man?" replies her father. "Well, may the best man win." At once you reply, "Ha! Ha! Ha!" He then says, "Is this your first visit to

Chicago?" to which the correct answer is, "Yes, sir, but I hope it isn't my last."

The bride's mother then appears. "This is my best man," says the groom. "Well," says she, "remember—the best man doesn't always win." "Ha! Ha! Ha!" you at once reply. "Is this your first visit to Chicago?" says she, to which you answer, "Yes—but I hope it isn't my last."

You are then conducted to your room, where you are left alone to unpack. In a few minutes the door will open and a small boy enter. This is the brother of the bride. You smile at him pleasantly and remark, "Is this your first visit to Chicago?" "What are you doing?" is his answer. "Unpacking," you reply. "What's that?" says he. "A cutaway," you reply. "What's that?" says he. "A collar bag." "What's that?" "A dress shirt." "What's that?" says he. "Another dress shirt." "What's that?" says he. "Say, listen," you reply, "don't I hear some one calling you?" "No," says he, "what's that?" "That," you reply, with a sigh of relief, "is a razor. Here

[53]

—take it and play with it." In three minutes, if you have any luck at all, the bride's brother will have cut himself severely in several places which will cause him to run crying from the room. You can then finish unpacking.

THE BRIDE'S TEA

THE first function of the pre-nuptial festivities is generally a tea at the bride's home, where the ushers and bridesmaids meet to become "acquainted." It is your duty, as best man, to go to the hotel where the ushers are stopping and bring them to this tea. Just as you will leave on this mission the groom will whisper in your ear, "For God's sake, remember to tell them that her father and mother are terribly opposed to drinking in any form." This is an awfully good joke on her father and mother.

As you step out of the hotel elevator you hear at the end of the hall a chorus shouting, "Mademoiselle from Armentières—*parlez vous!*" Those are your ushers.

Opening the door of the room you step for-

[54]

ward and announce, "Fellows, we have got
to go to a tea right away. Come on—let's go."
At this, ten young men in cutaways will stand
up and shout, "Yeaaa—the best man—give the
best man a drink!" From then on, at twelve
minute intervals, it is your duty to say, "Fellows, we have got to go to a tea right away.
Come on—let's go." Each time you will be
handed another drink, which you may take
with either your right or left hand.

After an hour the telephone will ring. It
will be the groom. He will say, "Everybody
is waiting for you and the ushers," to which
you reply, "We are just leaving." He then
says, "And don't forget to tell them what I
told you about her father and mother."

You then hang up the receiver, take a drink
in one hand and say, "Fellows, I have a very
solemn message for you. It's a message which
is of deep importance to each one of us. Fellows—her father and mother object to the use
of alcohol in any form."

This statement will be greeted with applause
and cheers. You will all then take one more

[55]

drink, put on your silk hats and gray gloves, and leave the room singing, "Her father and mother object to drink—*parlez vous.*"

The tea given by the bride's parents is generally a small affair to which only the members of the wedding party are invited. When you and the ushers arrive, you will find the bride, the maid of honor and the bridesmaids waiting for you. As you enter the room, make a polite bow to the bride's father and mother, and be sure to apologize for your lateness. Nothing so betrays the social "oil can" as a failure to make a plausible excuse for tardiness. Whenever you are late for a party you must always have ready some good reason for your fault, such as, "Excuse me, Mrs. Doe, I'm afraid I am a little late, but you see, just as I was dressing, this filling dropped out of my tooth and I had to have it put back in." If the host and hostess seem to doubt your statement, it would be well to show them the recalcitrant filling in question, although if they are "well-bred" they will probably in most cases take you at your word.

THE MAID OF HONOR

YOU and the ushers will then be introduced to the bridesmaids and the maid of honor. As you meet this latter young lady, who is the bride's older sister and, of course, your partner for the remainder of the wedding festivities, she will say, "The best man? Well, they say that the best man wins . . . Ha! Ha! Ha!" This puts her in class G 6 without further examination, and your only hope of prolonging your life throughout the next two days lies in the frequent and periodic administration of stimulants.

THE BACHELOR DINNER AND AFTER

THAT evening the groom gives for the best man and the ushers what is known as a "bachelor dinner." It is his farewell to his men friends as he passes out of the state of bachelorhood. The formal passing out generally occurs toward the end of the dinner, and is a quaint ceremony participated in by most of those present.

[57]

It is customary for the best man to wake up about noon of the following day. You will not have the slightest idea as to where you are or how you got there. You will be wearing your dress trousers, your stiff or pleated bosom dress shirt, black socks and pumps, and the coat of your pajamas. In one hand you will be clutching a chrysanthemum. After a few minutes there will come a low moan from the next bed. That is usually the groom, also in evening dress with the exception that he has tried to put on the trousers of your pajamas over his dress trousers. You then say, "What happened?" to which he replies, "Oh, Judas." You wait several minutes. In the next room you hear the sound of a shower bath and some one whistling. The bath stops; the whistling continues. The door then opens and there enters one of the ushers. He is the usher who always "feels great" the next day after the bachelor dinner. He says to you, "Well, boys, you look all in." You do not reply. He continues, "Gosh, I feel fine." You make no response. He then begins to chuckle, "I don't suppose you remember," he says, "what you said to the bride's mother when I brought you home last night." You sit quickly up in bed. "What did I say?" you ask. "Was I tight?" "Were you tight?" he replies, still chuckling. "Don't you remember what you said? And don't you remember trying to get the bride's father to slide down the banisters with you? Were you tight—Oh, my gosh!" He then exits, chuckling. Statistics of several important life insurance companies show that that type of man generally dies a violent death before the age of thirty.

THE REHEARSAL

THE rehearsal for the wedding is usually held in the church on the afternoon preceding the day of the nuptials. The ushers, of course, are an hour late, which gives the bridegroom (Bap.) an opportunity to meet the minister (Epis.) and have a nice, long chat about religion, while the best man (Atheist) talks to the eighty-three year old sexton who buried the bride's grandpa and grandma and has

[59]

knowed little Miss Dorothy come twenty
years next Michaelmas. The best man's offer
of twenty-five dollars, if the sexton will at once
bury the maid of honor, is generally refused as
a matter of courtesy.

THE BRIDAL DINNER

IN the evening, the parents of the bride give
the bridal dinner, to which all the relatives
and close friends of the family are invited.
Toasts are drunk in orange juice and rare old
Virginia Dare wine, and much good-natured
fun is indulged in by all. Speeches are usually made by the bride and groom, their parents, the best man, the maid of honor, the
minister and Aunt Harriet.

Just a word about the speeches at a bridal
dinner. Terrible!

A CHURCH WEDDING

ON the day of the wedding the ushers
should arrange to be at the church an
hour or so in advance of the time set for the
ceremony. They should be dressed in cuta-

ways, with ties, gloves and gardenias provided by the groom.

It is the duty of the best man to dress the bridegroom for the wedding. As you enter his room you see, lying half-dressed on the bed, a pale, wan, emaciated creature, who is staring fixedly at the ceiling. It is the happy bridegroom. His lips open. He speaks feebly. "What time is it?" he says. You reply, "Two-thirty, old man. Time to start getting dressed." "Oh, my God!" says the groom. Ten minutes pass. "What time is it?" says the groom. "Twenty of three," you reply. "Here's your shirt." "Oh, my God!" says the groom.

He takes the shirt and tries to put it on. You help him. "Better have a little Scotch, old man," you say. "What time is it?" he replies. "Five of three," you say. "Oh, my God!" says the groom.

At three-thirty you and he are dressed in cutaways and promptly at three-forty-two you arrive at the church. You are ushered into a little side room where it is your duty to sit

[61]

with the corpse for the few brief hours which elapse between three-forty-five and four o'clock. Occasionally he stirs and a faint spark of life seems to struggle in his sunken eyes. His lips move feebly. You bend over to catch his dying words. "Have—you—got —the ring?" he whispers. "Yes," you reply. "Everything's fine. You look great, too, old man." The sound of the organ reaches your ears. The groom groans. "Have you got the ring?" he says.

Meanwhile the ushers have been performing their duty of showing the invited guests to the various pews. A correctly trained usher will always have ready some cheery word or sprightly bit of conversation to make the guests feel perfectly at home as he conducts them to their seats. "It's a nice day, isn't it?" is suggested as a perfectly safe and yet not too unusual topic of conversation. This can be varied by remarking, "Isn't it a nice day?" or in some cases, where you do not wish to appear too forward, "Is it a nice day, or isn't it?" An usher should also remember that

[62]

The man of culture and refinement, while always considerate to those beneath him in station, never, under any circumstances, loses control of his emotions for an instant. Though the gentleman-rider in the picture may be touchingly fond of his steeplechase horse, it is unpardonably bad form for him to make an exhibition of his affection while going over the brush in plain view of numbers of total strangers. In doing so he simply is making a "guy" of himself, and it is no more than he deserves if those in the gallery raise their eyebrows at each other and smile knowingly.

The Romans had a proverb, "Litera scripta manet," which means "The written letter remains." The subtle wisdom of these words was no doubt well known to the men of the later Paleolithic Age before them, but evidently the gentleman in the engraving never heard of it. If he had kept this simple little rule of social correspondence in mind he would have avoided the painful experience of hearing his obsolete emotions exposed to the eager ears of twelve perfect strangers. It is customary nowadays for unmarried elder sons of our most aristocratic families to express their appreciation of the qualities of fascinating bachelor girls over the sensible, though plebeian, telephone.

although he has on a cutaway, he is neither a floor-walker nor a bond salesman, and remarks such as "Something in a dotted Swiss?" or "Third aisle over—second pew—next the ribbon goods," are decidedly *non au fait.*

The first two pews on each side of the center aisle are always reserved for members of the immediate family, but it is a firmly established custom that the ushers shall seat in these "family pews" at least three people with whom the family are barely on speaking terms. This slight error always causes Aunt Nellie and Uncle Fred to sit up in the gallery with the family cook.

With the arrival of the bride, the signal is given to the organist to start the wedding march, usually either Mendelssohn's or Wagner's. About this time the mother of the bride generally discovers that the third candle from the left on the rear altar has not been lighted, which causes a delay of some fifteen minutes during which time the organist improvises one hundred and seventy-three variations on the opening strains of the march.

[63]

Finally all is adjusted and the procession starts down the aisle led by the ushers swaying slowly side by side. It is always customary for three or four of the eight ushers to have absolutely no conception of time or rhythm, which adds a quaint touch of uncertainty and often a little humor to the performance.

After the Scotch mist left by the passing ushers has cleared, there come the bridesmaids, the maid of honor, and then, leaning on her father's arm (unless, of course, her father is dead), the bride.

In the meantime, the bridegroom has been carried in by the best man and awaits the procession at the foot of the aisle, which is usually four hundred and forty yards long. The ushers and bridesmaids step awkwardly to one side; the groom advances and a hush falls over the congregation which is the signal for the bride's little niece to ask loudly, "What's that funny looking man going to do, Aunt Dotty?"

Then follows the religious ceremony.

Immediately after the church service, a re-

ception is held at the bride's home, where refreshments are served and two hundred and
forty-two invited guests make the same joke
about kissing the bride. At the reception it
is customary for the ushers and the best man
to crawl off in separate corners and die.

The wedding "festivities" are generally concluded with the disappearance of the bride,
the bridegroom, one of the uninvited guests
and four of the most valuable presents.

Chapter Three

THE ETIQUETTE
OF TRAVEL

CHAPTER THREE: THE ETIQUETTE OF TRAVEL

THE etiquette of travel, like that of courtship and marriage, has undergone several important changes with the advent of "democracy" and the "mechanical age." Time was when travel was indulged in only by the better classes of society and the rules of travellers' etiquette were well defined and acknowledged by all. But Yankee ingenuity has indeed brought the "mountain to Mahomet"; the "iron horse" and the "Pullman coach" have, I believe, come to stay, bringing with them many new customs and manners for the well-bred gentleman or lady who would travel correctly. Truly, the "old order changeth" and it is, perhaps, only proper that one should keep (if you will pardon the use of the word) "abreast" of the times.

[69]

Perfect Behavior

HINTS FOR THE CORRECT PEDESTRIAN

LET us suppose, for example, that you are a young gentleman of established social position in one of the many cities of our great middle west, and it is your desire to travel from your home to New York City for the purpose of viewing the many attractions of that metropolis of which I need perhaps only mention the Aquarium or Grant's Tomb or the Eden Musée. Now there are many ways of getting to New York, such as (a) on foot, (b) via "rail"; it should be your first duty to select one of these methods of transportation. Walking to New York ("a" above) is often rejected because of the time and effort involved and it is undoubtedly true that if one attempted to journey afoot from the middle west one would probably be quite fatigued at the end of one's journey. The etiquette of walking, however, is the same for short as for long distances, and I shall at this point give a few of the many rules for correct behavior among pedestrians.

[70]

The Etiquette of Travel

In the first place, it is always customary in a city for a young lady, either accompanied or unaccompanied, to walk on the sidewalk. A young "miss" who persists in walking in the gutters is more apt to lose than to make friends among the socially "worth while."

Gentlemen, either with or without ladies, are never seen walking after dark in the sewers or along the elevated tracks.

It is not *au fait* for gentlemen or ladies wearing evening dress to "catch on behind" passing ice wagons, trucks, etc.; the time and energy saved are doubtfully repaid should one happen to be driven thus past other members of one's particular social "set."

Ladies walking alone on the street after dark do not speak to gentlemen unless they have been previously introduced or are out of work with winter coming on.

A gentleman walking alone at night, when accosted by a young woman whom he has not met socially, removes his hat politely, bows and passes on, unless she looks awfully good.

Débutantes meeting traffic policemen al-

[71]

ways bow first in America; in the Continental countries, with their age-old flavor of aristocratic court life, this custom is reversed.

A bachelor, accompanied by a young unmarried woman, when stepping accidentally into an open coal or sewer hole in the sidewalk, removes his hat and gloves as inconspicuously as possible.

It is never correct for young people of either "sex" to push older ladies in front of swiftly approaching motor vehicles or street cars.

A young man, if run over by an automobile driven by a strange lady, should lie perfectly still (unless dead) until an introduction can be arranged; the person driving the car usually speaks first.

An unmarried woman, if run into and knocked down by a taxicab driven by someone in her own "set," usually says "Why the hell don't you look where you're going?" to which the taxi driver, removing his hat, replies "Why the hell don't *you?*"

A correct costume for gentlemen walking in the parks or streets of a city, either before or after dark, consists of shoes (2), socks (2), undergarments, trousers, shirt, necktie, collar, vest, coat and hat. For pedestrians of the "opposite" sex the costume is practically the same with the exception of the socks, trousers, shirt, necktie, collar, vest and coat. However, many women now affect "knickerbockers" and *vice versa*.

A young lady of good breeding, when walking alone, should not talk or laugh in a loud boisterous manner. "Capers" (e. g. climbing trees, etc.), while good exercise and undoubtedly fashionable in certain "speedy" circles, are of questionable taste for ladies, especially if indulged in to excess or while walking with young gentlemen on the Sabbath. Sport is sport, and no one loves a stiff game of "fives" or "rounders" more than I, but the spectacle of a young unmarried lady and her escort hanging by their limbs on the Lord's Day from the second or third cross arm of an electric telegraph pole is certainly carrying things a bit too far, in my opinion, even in this age of "golf" and lawn "tennis."

[73]

Perfect Behavior

A young gentleman escorting a young lady on foot to a formal ball or the opera should walk on the outside, especially if they are both in evening dress and have a long distance to go. It is never incorrect to suggest the use of a street car, or as one gets near the Opera House, a carriage or a "taxicab."

A young man walking with a young lady, when accosted by a beggar, always gives the beggar something unless the young lady is his wife or his sister.

So much for pedestrians. I can not, of course, pretend to give here all the rules for those who "go afoot" and I can only say that the safest principle for correct behavior in this, as in many social matters, is the now famous reply Thomas Edison once made to the stranger who asked him with what he mixed his paints in order to get such marvellous effects. "One part inspiration," replied the great inventor, "and *nine* parts perspiration." In other words, etiquette is not so much a matter of "genius" as of steady application to small details.

The Etiquette of Travel

TRAVELLING BY RAIL

IN America much of the travelling is done by "rail." The etiquette of railroad behavior is extremely complicated, especially if one is forced to spend the night *en route* (on the way) and many and ludicrous are the mistakes made by those whose social training has apparently fitted them more for a freight car than for an up-to-date "parlor" or "Pullman" coach.

GOOD FORM ON A STREET CAR

LET us, first of all, however, take up some of the simpler forms of rail transportation, such as, for example, the electric street or "tram" car now to be seen on the main highways and byways of all our larger cities. The rules governing behavior on these vehicles often appear at first quite complicated, but when one has learned the "ropes," as they say in the Navy, one should have no difficulty.

An elderly lady with a closed umbrella, for example, desiring to take a street car, should always stand directly under a large sign marked "Street Cars Do Not Stop On This Corner." As the car approaches she should run quickly out to the car tracks and signal violently to the motorman with the umbrella. As the car whizzes past without stopping she should cease signalling, remark "Well I'll be God damned!" and return to the curbstone. After this performance has been repeated with three successive cars she should then walk slowly out and lie down, in a dignified manner, across the car tracks. In nine cases out of ten the motorman of the next "tram" will see her lying there and will be gentleman enough to stop his car.

When this happens the elderly lady should get quietly up from the street and stand outside the door marked "Exit Only" until the motorman opens it for her. She should then enter with the remark, "I signalled to three cars and not one of them stopped," to which the motorman will reply, "But, lady, that sign there says they don't stop on this corner." The

The Etiquette of Travel

lady should then say "What's your number—
I'm going to report you."

After taking his number she should enter
the car. At the opposite end of the vehicle
there will undoubtedly be three or four vacant
seats; instead of taking one of these she should
stand up in front of some young man and
glare at him until he gets up and gives her
his place.

It is not customary in American cities for
ladies to thank gentlemen who provide them
with seats.

After a few minutes she should turn to the
man at her right and ask "Does this car go to
Madison Heights?" He will answer "No."
She should then turn to the man on her left
and ask "Does this car go to Madison
Heights?" He will answer "No." Her next
question—"Does this car go to Madison
Heights?"—should be addressed to a man
across the aisle, and the answer will be "No."
She should then listen attentively while the
conductor calls out the names of the streets and
as he shouts "Blawmnoo!" she should ask the

[77]

man at her right "Did he say Madison Heights?" He will reply "No." At the next street the conductor will shout "Blawmnoo!" at which she should ask "Did he say Madison Heights?" Once more the answer will be in the negative. The car will proceed, the conductor will now call "Blawmnoo!" and as the elderly lady once more says "Did he say Madison Heights?" the man at her left, the man at her right, the man across the aisle and eight other male passengers will shout "YES!"

It is then correct for her to pick up her umbrella and, carefully waiting until the conductor has pulled the "go ahead" signal, she should cry "Wait a minute, conductor—I want to get off here." The car will then be stopped and she should say "Is this Madison Heights?" to which the conductor will reply "This ain't the Madison Heights car, lady." She should then say "But you called out Madison Heights," to which he will answer "No, lady—that's eight miles in the opposite direction." She should then leave the street car,

[78]

Her conduct has stamped the young lady as a
provincial and it is not to be wondered at if sup-
pressed titters and half audible chuckles follow
her about the room. PERFECT BEHAVIOR would
have taught her that it is not the prerogative of a
muddy-complexioned dud—even if she has had only
one dance and her costume is very expensive—to
cut in on a gentleman (by grabbing his neck or
any other method) when he is dancing with the
wide-eyed beauty from the South who leaves in five
minutes to catch a train. He will be within his
rights when, at the end of five minutes, after three
unsuccessful attempts to loosen her grip, he will
carry her into the garden under false pretences and
there play the hose on her until she drowns.

They are leaving the home of an intimate friend of several weeks' standing, after having witnessed a Private Theatrical. Both feel that some return should be made for their hostess's kindness but neither is certain as to just what form the return should take. The Book of PERFECT BEHAVIOR *would have pointed out to them that the only adequate and satisfactory revenge for this sort of thing is to invite the lady, as soon as possible without exciting her suspicion, to attend an Italian opera or a drawing-room musicale.*

not forgetting, however, to take the conductor's number.

The above hints for "tram" car etiquette apply, of course, only to elderly ladies. For young men and women the procedure would be in many cases quite different. A young married woman, for example, on entering a street car, should always have her ticket or small "change" so securely buried in the fourth inside pocketbook of her handbag that she cannot possibly find it inside of twelve minutes. Three or more middle-aged ladies, riding together, should never decide as to who is to pay the fare until the conductor has gone stark raving mad.

IN THE SUBWAY

THE rules governing correct behavior in the underground "subway" systems of our great cities (particularly the New York subways) are, however, much more simple and elemental than the etiquette for surface cars. In the subway, for example, if you are a married man and living with your wife, or

[79]

head of a family, i. e., a person who actually supports one or more persons living in (or under) his (or her) household on the last day of the preceding calendar year, provided that such person or persons shall not on or before July 1 or if July 1 shall fall on a Sunday then on the day nearest preceding July 1, himself (or themselves) have filed a separate report as provided in paragraph (g), you should precede a lady when entering, and follow a lady when leaving, the train.

A HONEYMOON IN A SUBWAY

ON the other hand, a wedding or a "honeymoon" trip in a subway brings up certain problems of etiquette which are entirely different from the above. Let us suppose, for example, that the wedding takes place at high noon in exclusive old "Trinity" church, New York. The nearest subway is of course the "Interborough" (West Side) and immediately after the ceremony the lucky couple can run poste haste to the "Battery" and board a Lenox Ave. Local. Arriving at romantic Chambers

St. they should change at once to a Bronx Park Express which will speedily whizz them past 18th St., 23rd St. and 28th St. to the Pennsylvania Station where they can again transfer, this time to a Broadway Local. In a jiffy and two winks of an eye they will be at Times Square, the heart of the "Great White Way" (that Mecca of pleasure seekers and excitement lovers) where they can either change to a Broadway Express, journeying under Broadway to historic Columbia University and Harlem, or they can take the busy little "shuttle" which will hurry them over to the Grand Central Station. There they can board the aristocratic East Side Subway, either "up" or "down" town. The trip "up town" (Lexington Ave. Express) passes under some of the better class residential districts, but the journey in the other direction is perhaps more interesting, including as it does such stops as 14th St., Brooklyn Bridge, Fulton Street, Wall Street (the financial center) etc., not to mention a delightful passage under the East River to Brooklyn, the city of homes and

[81]

churches. Thus without getting out of their seats the happy pair can be transported from one fascinating end of the great city to the other and when they have exhausted the possibilities of a honeymoon in the Interborough they can change, with the additional cost of only a few cents apiece, to the B. R. T. or the Hudson Tubes which will gladly carry them to a thousand new and interesting places—a veritable Aladdin's lamp on rails.

TRAVELLING UNDER STEAM

AND now we come to that most complex form of travel—the railroad journey. Let us suppose that instead of attempting to walk to New York you have elected to go on the "train." On the day of your departure you should carefully pack your bag or suitcase, taking care to strap and lock it securely. You can then immediately unstrap and unlock it in order to put in the tooth paste and shaving brush which you forgot to bring from the bathroom.

Arriving at the station promptly on the time

scheduled for the train to depart you will find that because of "daylight saving time" you have exactly an hour to wait. The time, however, can be amusingly and economically spent in the station as follows: 11 weighing machines @ .01 = .11; 3 weighing machines @ .05 = .15; 1 weighing machine (out of order) .09; 17 slot machines (chocolate and gum) @ .01 = .17. Total cost—.50, unless, of course, you eat the chocolate.

Upon the arrival of the train you consult your ticket to find that you have "lower 9" in car 43. Walking back to the end of the train and entering car 43 you will find, in berth number 9, a tired woman and two small children. You will also find a hat box, a bird cage, a bag of oranges, a bag of orange peelings, a shoe-box of lunch, a rag doll, a toy balloon, half a "cookie" and 8,000,000 crumbs. The tired woman will then say to you "Are you the gentleman who has the lower berth?" to which you answer "Yes." She will then say "Well say—we've got the upper—and I wonder if you would mind—" "Not at all,"

[83]

you reply, "I should be only too glad to give you my lower." This is always done.

After you have seated yourself and the train has started the lady's little boy will announce, "I want a drink, Mama." After he has repeated this eleven times his mother will say to you "I wonder if you would mind holding the baby while I take Elmer to get a drink?"

The etiquette of holding babies is somewhat difficult for bachelors to master at first as there are no hard and fast rules governing conduct under these circumstances. An easy "hold" for beginners and one which is difficult for the ordinary baby to break consists in wrapping the left and right arms firmly around the center of the child, at the same time clutching the clothing with the right hand and the toes with the left and praying to God that the damn thing won't drop.

In this particular case, after Elmer and his mother have gone down the aisle after a drink, the baby which you are holding will at once begin to cry. Now as every mother knows, and especially those mothers who have had children, a baby does not cry without some specific reason and all that is necessary in the present instance is to discover this reason. First of all, the child may be merely hungry, in which case you should at once ask the porter to bring you the à la carte menu. You should then carefully go over the list of dishes with the infant, taking care to spell out and explain such names as he may not understand. "How would you like some nice assorted hors d'œuvres?" you say. "Waaaaa!" says the baby. "No hors d'œuvres," you say to the waiter. "Some blue points, perhaps—you know, o-y-s-t-e-r-s?" You might even act out a blue point or two, as in charades, so that the child will understand what you mean. In case, however, the baby does not cease crying after having eaten the first three or four courses, you should not insist on a salad and a dessert, for probably it is not hunger which is occasioning the outcry. Perhaps it is a pin, in which case you should at once bend every effort to the discovery and removal of the irritant. The most generally accepted modern

[85]

way of effecting this consists in passing a large electro-magnet over every portion of the child's anatomy and the pin (if pin there be) will of course at once come to light. Then, too, many small children cry merely because they have swallowed something which does not agree with them, such as, for example, a gold tooth or a shoe horn; the remedy in this case consists in *immediately* feeding the child the proper counter irritant. There is, really, no great mystery about the successful raising of children and with a few common sense principles, such as presented above, any mother may relieve herself of a great deal of useless anxiety. I hope I may be pardoned for a digression here, but I feel very strongly that "today's babies are tomorrow's citizens" and I do want to see them brought up in the proper way.

But to return to our train. Perhaps by this time the mother and Elmer will have returned and you will be relieved of further investigation as to the cause of the infant's discomfort. A few minutes later, however, little Elmer

[86]

will say "Mama, I want the window open."
This request will be duly referred to you via
the line of authority. It is then your duty to
assume a firm upright stance, with the weight
evenly distributed on both feet, and work for
twelve minutes and thirty-nine seconds in a
terrific struggle to raise the windows. At
the end of twelve minutes and forty seconds
you will succeed, the window will slowly go
up, and the train will at once enter a tunnel,
filling the car and you with coal smoke. In
the resulting darkness and confusion you
should seize little Elmer, throw him quickly
out of the open window and make your escape
to the gentlemen's smoking compartment in
the rear of your car.

In the "smoker" you will find three men.
The first of these will be saying "and he told
me that a bootlegger he knew had cleaned up
a thousand dollars a week since January."
The second will say "Well down where I
come from there's men who never took a drink
before prohibition who get drunk all the time

[87]

now." The third will say "Well, I tell you, men—the saloon had to go."

Provision for satisfying the "inner man" is now a regular part of the equipment of all modern trains, and about 6:30 or 7 you should leave your companions in the "smoker" and walk through the train until you reach the "diner." Here you will seat yourself at a table with three other gentlemen, the first of whom will be remarking, as you sit down, "and I know for a fact that this bootlegger is making over fifty thousand dollars a year."

A CORRECT NIGHT IN A PULLMAN

BEFORE the days of modern railroads one could not very well travel over night but now, thanks to Mr. Pullman, it is possible for the traveller to go to bed en route and be every bit as snug and comfortable as the proverbial insect in a rug. Shortly after dinner the porter will "make up" the berths in the car and when you desire to retire for the night you should ask him to bring you the ladder in order that you may ascend to upper 9. While

[88]

you are waiting you should stand in the aisle
and remove your coat, vest and shoes, and then
begin to search for your suitcase which you
will finally locate by crawling on your chin
and stomach under berth number 11. When
you again resume an upright position the train
will give a sudden lurch, precipitating you into
berth number 12. A woman's voice will then
say "Alice?" to which you should of course
answer "No" and climb quickly up the ladder
into your proper berth.

A great deal of "to do" is often made of the
difficulty involved in undressing in an upper
berth but most of this is quite uncalled for.
Experienced travellers now generally wait
until the lights of the car have been dimmed
or extinguished when the disrobing can be
done quite simply in five counts, as follows:
One—unloosen all clothing and lie flat on the
back. The respiration should be natural, easy
and through the lungs. The muscles should
be relaxed; *Two*—pivoting on the back of the
head and neck, inhale quickly, at the same time
drawing the muscles of the legs and arms

[89]

sharply under the body, as for a spring; *Three*—spring suddenly upward and to the right (or left), catching the bell cord (which extends along the roof of the train) with the teeth, hands and feet; *Four*—holding firmly to the cord with the knees, describe a sudden arc downward with the head and body, returning to position as soon as the shirt and undershirt have dropped off into the aisle; *Five* —taking a firm hold on the cord with the teeth, let go sharply with the knees. The trousers, etc., should at once slide off, and you can (and, in fact, should) then swing yourself quickly back into your berth and pajamas.

Once inside your "bunk" you should drift quickly off to slumberland, and when you wake up it will be five minutes later and the —— —— engineer will be trying to see what he can do with an air brake and a few steel sleeping cars.

In the morning you will be in New York.

Chapter Four

AT THE CONCERT
AND THE OPERA

CHAPTER FOUR: At the Concert and the Opera

IN order to listen to music intelligently—or what is really much more important—in order to give the appearance of listening to music intelligently, it is necessary for the novice to master thoroughly two fundamental facts.

The first, and most important of these, is that the letter "w" in Russian is pronounced like "v"; the second, that Rachmaninoff has a daughter at Vassar.

Not very difficult, surely—but it is remarkable how much enjoyment one can get out of music by the simple use of these two formulas. With a little practise in their use, the veriest tyro can bewilder her escort even though she be herself so musically uninformed as to think that the celeste is only used in connection with

Aïda, or that a minor triad is perhaps a young wood nymph.

One other important fundamental is that enthusiasm should never be expressed for any music written after 1870; by a careful observance of this rule one will constantly experience that delightful satisfaction which comes with finding one's opinions shared by the music critics in the daily press.

LISTENING TO A SYMPHONY ORCHESTRA

THE first thing to do on arriving at a symphony concert is to express the wish that the orchestra will play Beethoven's Fifth. If your companion then says "Fifth what?" you are safe with him for the rest of the evening; no metal can touch you. If, however, he says "So do I"—this is a danger signal and he may require careful handling.

The next step is a glance at the program. If your escort is quite good looking and worth cultivating, the obvious remark is "Oh dear— not a very interesting program, to-night. But George—*look* at what they are playing next

The young lady in the picture has just laid out a perfect drive. She had, unfortunately, neglected to wait until the gentleman playing ahead of her had progressed more than fifteen yards down the fairway, and her ball, traveling at a velocity of 1675 f.s., has caught the gentleman squarely in the half-pint bottle. What mistake, if any, is the gentleman making in chasing her off the course with his niblick, if we assume that she called "Fore!" when the ball had attained to within three feet of the gentleman?

You will exclaim, no doubt, on looking at the scene depicted above, "Cherchez la femme." It is, however, nothing so serious as you will pardonably suppose. The gentleman is merely an inexperienced "gun" at a shooting-party, who has begun following his bird before it has risen above the head of his loader. This very clumsy violation of the etiquette of sport proves, beyond the shadow of a doubt, that he has learned to shoot from the comic papers, and that his coat-of-arms can never again be looked upon as anything but bogus.

Thursday! My, I wish—." If George shies at this, it can be tried again later—say during an "appassionato" passage for the violins and cellos.

As soon as the music starts, all your attention should be directed toward discovering someone who is making a noise—whispering or coughing; having once located such a creature, you should immediately "sh-sh" him. Should he continue the offence, a severe frown must accompany the next "sh-sh," a lorgnette —if available—adding great effectiveness to the rebuke. This will win you the gratitude of your neighbors and serve to establish your position socially, as well as musically—for perfect "sh-shers" do not come from the lower classes.

At the conclusion of the first number the proper remark is "hmmm," accompanied by a slow shake of the head. After this you may use any one of a number of remarks, as for example, "Well, I suppose Mendelssohn appeals to a great many people," or "That was meaningless enough to have been written by a

Russian." This latter is to be preferred, for it leads your companion to say, "But don't you like TschaiKOWsky?", pronouncing the second syllable as if the composer were a female bull. You can then reply, "Why, yes, TschaiKOFFsky *did* write some rather good music—although it's all neurotic and obviously Teutonic." Don't fail to stress the "v."

The next number on the program will probably be the soloist—say, a coloratura soprano. Your first remark should be that you don't really care for the human voice—the reason being, of course, that symphonic music, ABSOLUTE music, has spoiled you for things like vocal gymnastics. This leads your bewildered friend to ask you what sort of soloist you prefer.

Ans.—Why, a piano concerto, of course.

Ques.—And who is your favorite pianist?

Ans.—Rachmaninoff.

And then, before the boy has time to breathe—SHOOT! *"Did you know that he has a daughter at Vassar?"*

Although not necessary, it might be well to

[96]

finish off the poor fellow at the end of the concert with one or two well placed depth bombs. My own particular favorite for this is the following, accompanied by a low sigh: "After all—Beethoven IS Beethoven."

CORRECT BEHAVIOR AT A PIANO RECITAL

THE same procedure is recommended for the piano or violin recital, with the possible addition of certain phrases such as "Yes —of course, she has technique—but, my dear, so has an electric piano." This remark gives you a splendid opportunity for sarcasm at the expense of Mr. Duo-Art and other manufacturers of mere mechanical perfection; the word "soul"—pronounced with deep feeling, as when repeating a fish order to a stupid waiter—may be introduced effectively several times.

The program at these recitals is likely to be more complex than that at a symphony concert. This is a distinct advantage, for it gives you a splendid opportunity to catch some wretch applauding before the music is really

[97]

finished. Nothing is quite comparable to the satisfaction of smiling knowingly at your neighbors when this *faux pas* is committed, unless it be the joy of being the first to applaud at the *real* conclusion. This latter course, however, is fraught with danger for the beginner; the chances for errors in judgment are many, and the only sure way to avoid anachronistic applause is to play the safe game and refrain altogether from any expression of approval—a procedure which is heartily recommended for the musically ignorant, it being also the practise among the majority of the critics.

IN A BOX AT THE OPERA

THE opera differs from the symphony concert, or piano recital, in the same way that the army drill command of "At Ease!" differs from "Rest!" When one of these orders (I never could remember which) is given to a battalion in formation, it signifies that talking is permitted; opera, of course, corresponds to that command.

At the Concert and the Opera

Before the invention of the phonograph it was often necessary for the opera goer to pay some attention to the performance—at least while certain favorite arias were being sung; this handicap to the enjoyment of opera has now fortunately been overcome and one can devote one's entire attention to other more important things, safe in one's knowledge that one has Galli-Curci at home on the Vic.

In order really to get the most out of an opera a great deal of study and preparation is required in advance; I have not space at this time to cover these preliminaries thoroughly, but would recommend to the earnest student such supplemental information as can be obtained from Lady Duff-Gordon, or Messrs. Tiffany, Técla and Pinaud.

Upon entering one's box the true opera lover at once assumes a musical attitude; this should be practised at home, by my lady, before a mirror until she is absolutely sure that the shoulders and back can be seen from any part of the house. Then, with the aid of a pair of strong opera glasses, she may proceed to scru-

tinize carefully the occupants of the boxes—
noting carefully any irregular features. Tech-
nical phraseology, useful in this connection,
includes "unearthly creature," "stray leopard"
or, simply, "that person."

Your two magical formulas—the Russian
"w" and the sad story about Rachmaninoff's
daughter—may, of course, be held in reserve—
but the chances are that you will be unable to
use them, for during an evening at the opera
there will probably be no mention of music.

Chapter Five

ETIQUETTE FOR
DRY AGENTS

CHAPTER FIVE: ETIQUETTE FOR DRY AGENTS

SOME BROADER ASPECTS OF PROHIBITION

IN spite of the great pride and joy which we Americans feel over the success of National Prohibition; in spite of the universal popularity of the act and the method of its enforcement; in spite of the fact that it is now almost impossible to obtain in any of our ex-saloons anything in the least resembling whiskey or gin,—there still remains the distressing suspicion that quite possibly, at some of the dinner parties and dances of our more socially prominent people, liquor—or its equivalent—is openly being served. Dry agents have, of course, tried on several occasions to verify this suspicion; their praiseworthy efforts have met, for the most part, with scant success.

The main difficulty has been, I believe, that the average dry agent is too little versed in

[103]

the customs and manners of polite society. It is lamentably true that, too often, has a carefully planned society dry raid been spoiled because the host noticed that one of his guests was wearing white socks with a black tie, or that the intruder was using his dessert spoon on the hors d'œuvres.

The solution of this difficulty lies, of course, in the gradual procuring of a better class of dry agent. There are signs (though, unfortunately, in the wrong direction) that some of our younger college generation are already casting envious eyes toward the rich rewards, the social opportunities and the exciting life of the professional bootlegger.

It might be well to interest some of these promising youngsters in the no less exciting occupation of National Prohibition Enforcement Officer. At present the chief difficulty seems to lie in the fact that, in our preparatory schools and colleges, a young man acquires a certain code of honor which causes him to look with distaste on what he calls pussyfooting and sneaking.

Etiquette for Dry Agents

People too often forget that, in order to make effective such a universally beneficent law, any means are justified. It will be, I hope, only a matter of years before this distrust of the "sneak" will have died out, and the Dry Agent will come to be regarded with the reverence and respect due to one who devotes his life to the altruistic investigation of his neighbor's affairs.

THE COLLEGE GRADUATE AS DRY AGENT

THEN, too, many young college men are deterred from becoming Dry Agents by thinking of the comparative scantiness of the monetary rewards. This difficulty is only an imaginary one—for, luckily, as soon as a man's code of honor has been elevated to the extent that it permits him to take up a career of pussyfooting there is generally eliminated at the same time any objection he might have to what is often called bribery. Thus, by a fortunate combination of circumstances, a Dry Agent is enabled to serve mankind and, at the

[105]

same time, greatly increase his own personal fortune.

But we cannot wait until our college graduates come to regard pussyfooting as a career. We must do what we can with the material at our disposal. We must in some way educate our present Dry Agents so that they can go to any function in polite society and remain as inconspicuous and as completely disregarded as the host. As a first step in such a social training I offer the following suggestions, in the hope that before long no function will be complete without the presence of four or five correctly dressed National Prohibition Enforcement Officers, ready and eager to arrest the host and hostess and all the guests on the slightest provocation.

PLANNING A DRY RAID ON A MASQUERADE BALL

L ET us suppose, for example, that you are a Dry Agent and that your name is Isador Eisenberg, and, one day, you and your chief are sitting around the Dry Agent's Club and he says to you, "Izzy—I see by the paper that there's a swell society masquerade ball to be given by the younger married set tomorrow night at the Glen Cove Country Club. Take your squad to cover it." At this point you doubtless say, "Chief, I'm afraid I can't use my squad. My men have been disguised as trained seals all this week, and tomorrow night, they are to raid all the actresses' dressing rooms at the Hippodrome" and then the Chief says, "Well, Izzy, you'll have to rent a costume and pull off the raid all by yourself."

A WORD ABOUT CORRECT COSTUMES

YOUR first concern should be, of course, your costume. If you have a high voice (although really there is no reason for supposing that all Dry Agents have high voices), you might well attend the masquerade disguised as a lady. One of the neatest and, on the whole, most satisfactory of ladies' disguises is that of Cleopatra. Cleopatra, as you know, was once Queen of Egypt and the costume is quite simple and attractive. It may be, however, that you would prefer to appear as a modern, rather than an ancient queen. A modern Queen (if one may judge from the illustrated foreign periodicals) always wears a plain suit and carries a tightly rolled umbrella. Should you care to attend the masquerade as an allegorical figure—say "2000 Years of Progress"—you might wear the Cleopatra costume and carry the umbrella. Or you might go attired as some other less prominent member of the nobility—for instance, Lady Dartmouth, whose delightful costume is more or less featured in the advertising on our better class subways and street cars, and can be obtained at a comparatively small cost at any reliable dry goods store.

Should you, however, feel that you would be more at ease in a male costume, there are several suggestions which might cleverly conceal your real identity. You might, for example, attend the ball as Jurgen—a costume which would assure you a pleasurable evening and many pleasing acquaintances. You might, with equal satisfaction, go as an Indian.

Etiquette for Dry Agents

It occurs to me that it might even be a clever move to attend the party dressed as a Dry Agent. All suspicion would be instantly lost in the uproar of laughter which would greet your announcement of your disguise; many men would probably so far enter into the spirit of the joke as to offer you drinks from their flasks, and much valuable evidence could be obtained in this way. And the costume is quite easy—simply wear a pleated soft-bosom dress shirt with your evening dress, and tuck the ends of your black tie under your collar.

GOOD FORM FOR DRY AGENTS DURING A RAID

AFTER the costume, you should arrange to obtain a mask and a breath. The former is, of course, for the purpose of hiding your identity; the latter is essential at any party where you wish to remain inconspicuous. A good whisky breath can usually be obtained from a bottle of any of the better known brands of Scotch or Rye whisky by holding a small quantity of the liquor in the mouth for

[109]

a short period of time. It is not, of course, necessary to swallow the liquor and in this connection I would suggest that you use *only* the best grade whisky, for there are at present being manufactured for domestic consumption several brands which, if held in the mouth for a longer interval than, say, three seconds, are apt to eat away the tongue or dissolve several of your more important teeth.

On the night of the party, therefore, having donned your Dry Agent costume, having put on your mask, having secured a good breath— you jump into a taxicab and drive to the Glen Cove Country Club. And, as you enter the door of the club, some girl, dressed, probably, as Martha Washington, will run up and kiss you. This is not because she thinks you are George Washington; it is because she drank that eighth Bronx cocktail at dinner.

And right at this point is where most Dry Agents have displayed their ignorance of the usages of polite society, for most of them are wofully ignorant of the correct way to handle such a situation. Your average Dry Agent,

[110]

Packets of old letters, bits of verse, locks of hair, pressed flowers, inscribed books, photographs, etc., all make acceptable wedding gifts. By telling you whether they should be presented to the Bride or to the Groom PERFECT BEHAVIOR has, we feel, settled the question of future happiness in many a new-made home.

You are, let us say, one of the Ushers attending the Bachelor Dinner. You are handed a bottle of Chateau Lafitte '69. Can you select, from the diagram above, the proper implement to use in getting at its contents? The correct methods of choosing and using table hardware are explained in PERFECT BEHAVIOR.

The young couple in the picture are trying to word a plausible letter of regret in answer to an invitation to a house-party. Had they consulted their PERFECT BEHAVIOR they would have known that there is no plausible excuse for not accepting any invitation whatever, and that the simplest and most dignified method is to write the attached model letter.

not being accustomed to the ways of Younger Marrieds, is often confused upon being unexpectedly kissed, and in his confusion betrays his unfortunate lack of social training.

The correct way to meet the above situation is based on the fundamental rule of all social etiquette—common sense. Return the lady's kiss in an easy, natural manner and pass on. If she follows you, lead her at once to a quiet unoccupied corner of the club and knock her over the head with a chair or some other convenient implement. It has been found that this is the only effective way to deal with this type of woman and it is really only a kindness to her and her husband to keep her from embarrassing you with her attentions during the rest of the evening.

After you have removed your coat, you should go to the ball room where you will find the dance in full swing—full being of course used in its common or alcoholic sense. Take your place in the stag line and don't, under any circumstances, allow anyone to induce you to cut in on any of the dancers. In the

[III]

first place, you won't be able to dance because
Dry Agents, like Englishmen, never can; sec-
ondly, if you *try* to dance, you are taking the
enormous chance, especially at a masquerade,
that the man who introduced you to your partner will disappear for the rest of the evening,
leaving you with Somebody's Albatross hanging around your neck. And, of all Alba-
trosses, the married one is perhaps farthest
South—especially if she happens to be a little
tight and wants to talk about her husband and
children.

Your policy, therefore, should be one of
complete non-partisanship. If you do not
dance, do not let yourself be drawn into conversation, and do not, above all things, show
any consideration for the host or hostess. By
closely observing the actions of the men and
women about you, by wandering down into the
club bar, by peeking into the automobiles
parked outside the club, you will probably be
able to obtain sufficient evidence of the presence of alcohol to justify a raid. And then,
when you have raided the Glen Cove Country

Club, you can turn your attention to the 12,-635,439 other clubs and private houses where the same thing is going on. And, if Mr. Volstead has a dress suit, you might take him with you, and show him just how beautifully Prohibition is working and how enthusiastic the better classes of American society are about it.

Chapter Six

A CHAPTER FOR
SCHOOLGIRLS

CHAPTER SIX: A CHAPTER FOR SCHOOL-GIRLS

EVERY Fall a larger number of young girls leave home to come East to the various Finishing Schools in this section of the country. For the benefit of those who are making this trip for the first time, we outline a few of the more important points in connection with the preliminaries to the trip East, together with minute instructions as to the journey itself.

SELECTING A PROPER SCHOOL

THIS is, of course, mainly a parent's problem and is best solved by resorting to the following formula: Let A and B represent two young girls' finishing schools in the East. Mrs. Raleigh-Jones (X), from the West, sends her daughter to A; Mrs. Borax (Y), from the same city, sends her daughter to B. Upon consulting the local social register, it is found that Mr. Raleigh-Jones is a member of the Union, Colonial, Town and Country, and Valley Hunt Clubs; upon consulting the telephone directory it is found that the Boraxes live at 1217 S. Main Street, and that Mr. Borax is an undertaker. Shall Mrs. F. B. Gerald (Z) send her daughter Annette to A or to B, and why?

Answer: A, because life is real, life is earnest, and the grave is not its goal.

CORRECT EQUIPMENT FOR THE SCHOOLGIRL

HAVING selected an educational institution, the next requisite is a suitable equipment. Girls who live in other parts of the United States are often surprised to discover that the clothes which they have purchased at the best store in their home town are totally unsuited for the rough climate of the East. I would, therefore, recommend the fol-

[118]

lowing list, subject, of course, to variation in individual cases.

1 Dress, chine, crêpe de, pink, for dancing.
1 Dress, chine, crêpe de, pink, for petting.
1 Dress, Swiss, Dotted, blue, or
1 Dress, Swiss, undotted, white.
15 yards Tulle, best quality, pink.
4 bottles perfume, domestic, or
1 bottle, perfume, French.
12 Dozen Dorine, men's pocket size.
6 Soles, cami, assorted.
1 Brassière, or riding habit.
100 boxes aspirin, for dances and house-parties.
1 wave, permanent, for conversation.
24 waves, temporary.
10,000 nets, hair.
100,000 pins, hair.
1 bottle *Quelques Fleurs,* for knockout.

EN ROUTE

AFTER the purchase of a complete outfit, it will be necessary to say goodbye to one's local friends. Partings are always somewhat sad, but it will be found that much simple pleasure may be derived from the last nights with the various boys to whom one is engaged.

In this connection, however, it would be well to avoid making any rash statements regarding undying friendship and affection, because, when you next see Eddie or Walter, at Christmas time, you will have been three months in the East, while they have been at the State University, and really, after one starts dancing with Yale men—well, it's a funny world.

In case you do not happen to meet any friends on the train, the surest way to protect yourself from any unwelcome advances is to buy a copy of the *Atlantic Monthly* and carry it, in plain view. Next to a hare lip, this is the safest protection for a travelling young girl that I know of; it has, however, the one objection that all the old ladies on the train are likely to tell you what they think of Katherine Fullerton Gerould, or their rheumatism.

If you are compelled to go to the dining car alone, you will probably sit beside an Elk with white socks, who will call the waiter

"George." Along about the second course he will say to you, "It's warm for September, isn't it?" to which you should answer "No." That will dispose of the Elk.

Across the table from you will be a Grand Army man and his wife, going to visit their boy Elmer's wife's folks in Schenectady. When the fish is served, the Grand Army man will choke on a bone. Let him choke, but do not be too hopeful, as the chances are that he will dislodge the bone. All will go well until the dessert, when his wife will begin telling how raspberry sherbet always disagrees with her. Offer her your raspberry sherbet.

After dinner you may wish to read for a while, but the porter will probably have made up all the berths for the night. It will also be found that the light in your berth does not work, so you will be awake for a long time; finally, just as you are leaving Buffalo, you will at last get to sleep, and when you open your eyes again, you will be—in Buffalo.

There will be two more awakenings that

night—once at Batavia, where a merry wedding party with horns and cow bells will follow the lucky bride and groom into your car, and once at Schenectady, where the Pullman car shock-absorbing tests are held. The next morning, tired but unhappy, you will reach New York.

A JOURNEY AROUND NEW YORK

The Aquarium. Take Fifth Avenue Bus to Times Square. Transfer to 42nd Street Crosstown. Get off at 44th Street, and walk one block south to the Biltmore. The most interesting fish will be found underneath the hanging clock, near the telephone booths.

Grant's Tomb. Take Fifth Avenue bus, and a light lunch. Change at Washington Square to a blue serge or dotted Swiss. Ride to the end of the line, and walk three blocks east. Then return the same way you came, followed by three fast sets of tennis, a light supper and early to bed. If you do not feel better in the morning, cut out milk, fresh fruit and uncooked foods for a while.

Metropolitan Museum of Art. Take Subway to Brooklyn. (Flatbush.) Then ask the subway guard where to go; he will tell you.

The Bronx. Take three oranges, a lemon, three of gin, to one of vermouth, with a dash of bitters. Serve cold.

The Ritz. Take taxicab and fifty dollars. If you have only fifty dollars the filet of sole Marguéry is very good.

Brooklyn Bridge. Terrible. And their auction is worse.

When you have visited all these places, it will probably be time to take the train to your school.

THE FIRST DAYS IN THE NEW SCHOOL

THE first week of school life is apt to be quite discouraging, and we can not too emphatically warn the young girl not to do anything rash under the influence of home-

[123]

sickness. It is in this initial period that many girls, feeling utterly alone and friendless, write those letters to boys back home which are later so difficult to pass off with a laugh. It is during this first attack of homesickness also that many girls, in their loneliness, recklessly accept the friendship of other strange girls, only to find out later that their new acquaintance's mother was a Miss Gundlefinger of Council Bluffs, or that she lives on the south side of Chicago. We advise: Go slow at first.

BECOMING ACCLIMATIZED

IN your first day at school you will be shown your room; in your room you will find a sad-eyed fat girl. You will be told that this will be your room mate for the year. You will find that you have drawn a blank, that she comes from Topeka, Kan., that her paw made his money in oil, and that she is religious. You will be nice to her for the first week, because you aren't taking any chances at

[124]

the start; you will tolerate her for the rest of
the year, because she will do your lessons for
you every night.

Across the hall from you there will be two
older girls who are back for their second year.
One of them will remind you of the angel
painted on the ceiling of the Victory Theatre
back home, until she starts telling about her
summer at Narragansett; from the other you
will learn how to inhale.

A VISITOR FROM PRINCETON

ABOUT the middle of the first term your
cousin Charley Waldron, that freshman
at Princeton, will write and say that he would
like to come up and see you. You go to Miss
French and ask her if you can have your cousin
visit you. She sniffs at the "cousin" and tells
you that she must have a letter from Charley's
father, one from Charley's minister, one from
the governor of your state, and one from some
disinterested party certifying that Charley has
never been in the penitentiary, has never com-

mitted arson, and is a legitimate child. After you have secured these letters, Miss French will tell you that Charley will be allowed to see you next Saturday from four till five.

Charley will come and will be ushered into the reception room. While he is sitting there alone, the entire school will walk slowly, one by one, past the open door and look in at him. This will cause Charley to perspire freely and to wish to God he had worn his dark suit.

It is not at all likely that you will be allowed to go to New Haven during your first year, which is quite a pity, as this city, founded in 1638, is rich in historical interest. It was here, for example, in 1893, that Yale defeated Harvard at football, and the historic pigskin which was used that day is still preserved intact. Many other quaint relics are to be seen in and around the city of elms, mementos of the past which bring to the younger generation a knowledge and respect for things gone. In the month of June, for example, there is really nothing which quite conjures up for the college youth of today a sense of the mutability

"Who shall write first?" is a question that has perplexed many a lady or gentleman who is anxious to do the correct thing under any circumstances. A lady who has left town may send a brief note or a "P. P. C." ("pour prendre congé," i.e., "to take leave") card to a gentleman who remains at home, if the gentleman is her husband and if she has left town with his business partner.   Neither the note nor the card requires an acknowledgment, but many a husband takes pleasure in penning his congratulations to the lady, concluding with an expression of gratitude to his friend.

and impermanence of this mortal life so much as the sight of a member of the class of 1875 after three days' intensive drinking. *Eheu fugaces!*

Chapter Seven

THE ETIQUETTE OF GAMES AND SPORTS

CHAPTER SEVEN: THE ETIQUETTE OF GAMES AND SPORTS

GOLF AS A PASTIME

"GOLF" (from an old Scottish word meaning "golf") is becoming increasingly popular in the United States, and almost every city now has at least one private club devoted to the pursuit of this stylish pastime. Indeed, in many of our larger metropolises, the popular enthusiasm has reached such heights that free "public" courses have been provided for the citizens with, I may say, somewhat laughable results, as witness the fact that I myself have often seen persons playing on these "public" courses in ordinary shirts and trousers, tennis shoes, and *suspenders.*

The influence of this "democratization" on the etiquette of what was once an exclusive sport has been, in many instances, deplorable, and I am sure that our golf-playing fore-fathers would turn over in their graves were they to "play around" today on one of the "public" courses. In no pastime are the customs and unwritten laws more clearly defined, and it is essential that the young lady or gentleman of fashion who contemplates an afternoon on the "links" devote considerable time and attention to the various niceties of the etiquette of this ancient and honorable game.

A young man, for example, when playing with his employer, should always take pains to let his employer win. This is sometimes extremely difficult, but with practice even the most stubborn of obstacles can be overcome. On the first tee, for instance, after the employer, having swung and missed the ball completely one or two times, has managed to drive a distance of some forty-nine yards to the extreme right, the young man should take care to miss the ball completely *three* times, and then drive forty-eight yards to the extreme left. This is generally done by closing the eyes tightly and rising up sharply on both toes just before hitting the ball.

On the "greens" it is customary for a young man to "concede" his employer every "putt" which is within twenty feet of the hole. If the employer insists on "putting" [Ed. note:— He won't] and misses, the young man should take care to miss his own "putt." After both have "holed out," the young man should ask, "how many strokes, sir?" The employer will reply, "Let me see—I think I took seven for this hole, didn't I?" A well-bred young man will not under any circumstances remind his employer that he saw him use at least three strokes for the drive, three strokes for his second shot, four strokes in the "rough," seven strokes in the "bunker," and three "putts" on the "green," but will at once reply, "No, sir, I think you only took six, altogether." The employer will then say, "Well, well, call it six. I generally get five on this hole. What did you take?" The young man should then laugh cheerily and reply, "Oh, I took my customary seven." To which the employer will sympathetically say, "Too bad!"

After the employer has thus won his first three holes he will begin to offer the young man advice on how to improve his game. This is perhaps the most trying part of the afternoon's sport, but a young man of correct breeding and good taste will always remember the respect due an older man, and will not make the vulgar error of telling his employer for God's sake shut up before he gets a brassie in his —— —— ear.

A wife playing with her husband should do everything in her power to make the game enjoyable for the latter. She should encourage him, when possible, with little cheering proverbs, such as, "If at first you don't succeed, try, try again," and she should aid him with her advice when she thinks he is in need of it. Thus, when he drives into the sycamore tree on number eleven, she should say, "Don't you think, dear, that if you aimed a little bit more to the right. . . ." et cetera. When they come to number fourteen, and his second shot lands in the middle of the lake, she should remark, "Perhaps you didn't hit it hard enough, dear." And when, on the eighteenth, his approach goes through the second-story window of the club-house, she should say, "Dear, I wonder if you didn't hit that too hard?" Such a wife is a true helpmate, and not merely a pretty ornament on which a silly husband can hang expensive clothes, and if he is the right sort of man, he will appreciate this, and refrain from striking her with a niblick after this last remark.

A young wife who does not play the game herself can, nevertheless, be of great help to her husband by listening patiently, night after night, while he tells her how he drove the green on number three, and took a four on number eight (Par five), and came up to the fourteenth one under fours. Caddies should be treated at all times with the respect and pity due one's fellow creatures who are "unfortunate." The sins of the fathers are visited upon the children, and one should always remember that it is not, after all, the poor caddy's fault that he was born blind.

"CRAPS" is a game played with dice, which is often popular in the men's coat and smoking-rooms before and during formal receptions, balls, recitals, et cetera. It should not be imagined, however, that "craps" is a sport for men only; on the contrary, smart women are enthusiastically taking up this sport in numerous localities, and many an affair which started as a dinner party or a musicale has ended in a crap game, with all the guests seated in an excited circle on the floor, contributing to the host's efforts to make expenses for the evening.

It is in connection with these "mixed" games, however, that most of the more serious questions of "craps" etiquette arise. If, for example, you are a young man desirous of "shooting craps" with your grandmother, the correct way of indicating your desire when you meet the old lady in a public place is for you to remove your hat deferentially and say "Shoot a nickel, Grandmother?" If she wishes to play she will reply "Shoot, boy!" and you should then select some spot suitable for the game and assist her, if she wishes your aid, to kneel on the ground. It might be an added mark of gentility to offer her your handkerchief or coat upon which to rest her knees.

You should then take out the dice and "shoot." Your grandmother will look at your "throw" and say, "Oh, boy! He fives—he fives—a three and a two—never make a five—come on, you baby seven!" You should then take up the dice again and shake them in your right hand while your grandmother chants, "A four and a three—a five and a two—dicety dice, and an old black Joe—come on, you SEVEN!" You should then again "shoot." This time, as you have thrown a six and a one, your grandmother will then exclaim, "He sevens—the boy sevens—come on to grandmother, dice—talk to the nice old lady—

[137]

Perfect Behavior

Phoebe for grandma, dice, for grandpa needs a new pair of shoes—shoot a dime!"

She will then "throw," and so the game will go on until the old lady evidences a desire to stop, or, possibly, until either you or she are "cleaned out." In this latter case, however, it would be a customary act of courtesy towards an older person for you to offer to shoot your grandmother for her shawl or her side combs, thus giving her several more chances to win back the money she has lost. It should be recommended that young men never make a mistake in going a little out of their way on occasion to make life more pleasant and agreeable for the aged.

CORRECT BEHAVIOR ON A PICNIC

THERE often comes a time in the life of the members of "society" when they grow a little weary of the ceaseless round of teas, balls and dinners, and for such I would not hesitate to recommend a "picnic."

A day spent in the "open," with the blue sky over one's head, is indeed a splendid tonic for jaded nerves. But one should not make the mistake of thinking that because he (or she) is "roughing it" for a day, he (or she) can therefore leave behind his (or her) "manners," for such is not the case. There is a distinct etiquette for picnics, and any one who disregards this fact is apt to find to his (or her) sorrow that the "shoe" in this case is decidedly "on the other foot."

A young man, for example, is often asked by a young lady to accompany her on a "family picnic." To this invitation he should, after some consideration, reply either "Yes" or "No," and if the former, he should present himself at the young lady's house promptly on the day set for the affair (usually Sunday).

A "family picnic" generally consists of a Buick, a father, a mother, a daughter, a small son, beef loaf, lettuce sandwiches, a young man (you), two blow-outs, one spare tire, and Aunt Florence.

The father drives with his small boy beside him; in the rear are the mother, the daughter, Aunt Florence, the thermos bottles, the lunch baskets and you. As you take your seat you must remember that it is a distinct evidence of bad breeding to show in any way that you are conscious of the fact that the car has been standing for the last hour and forty-four minutes in the hot July sun.

"We're off!" cries father, pressing his foot on the self-starting pedal. Thirty minutes later you roll away from the curb and the picnic has begun. The intervening time has, of course, been profitably spent by you in walking to the nearest garage for two new spark-plugs.

It should be your duty, as guest, to see that the conversation in the rear seat is not allowed to lag. "It's a great day," you remark, as the car speeds along. "I think it's going to rain," replies Aunt Florence. "Not too fast, Will!" says mother. "Mother!" says the daughter.

Ten minutes later you should again remark, "My, what a wonderful day!" "Those clouds are gathering in the west," says Aunt Florence, "I think we had better put the top up." "I think this is the wrong road," says mother.

"Dear, I know what I'm doing," replies father.

The secret of good conversation lies in discovering the "hobby" of the person with whom one is conversing, and a good talker always throws out several "feelers" in order to find out the things in which his partner is most interested. You should, therefore, next say to mother, "Don't you think this is a glorious day for a picnic?" to which she will reply, "Well, I'm sure this is the wrong road. Hadn't you better ask?" The husband will answer nothing, but Aunt Florence will murmur, "I think I felt a drop of rain, Will. If you don't put the top up now, we'll all be drenched."

The husband will then stop the car, and you and he will proceed to put up the top. In doing this, it is customary for the guest to get the second and third fingers of his right hand so severely pinched that he can not use the hand for several days. As soon as the top is up and the rain curtains are in place the sun will come out and you can at once get out and put the top down, taking care this time to ruin two fingers of the *left* hand.

No good conversationalist confines himself exclusively to one subject, and when you are once more "under way" you should remark to the mother, "I think that motoring is great fun, don't you, Mrs. Caldwell?" Her answer will be, "I wish you wouldn't drive so fast!" You should then smile and say to Aunt Florence, "Don't *you* think that motoring is great fun, Mrs. Lockwood?" As she is about to reply, the left rear tire will blow out with a loud noise and the car will come to a bumping stop.

The etiquette of changing a tire is fairly simple. As soon as the "puncture" occurs one should at once remark, "Is there anything I can do?" This request should be repeated from time to time, always taking care, however, that no one takes it at all seriously. The real duty of a young man who is a "guest" on a motor trip on which a "blow-out" occurs is, of course, to keep the ladies of the party

Nowhere is the etiquette of travel more abused than in our subways. The gentleman shown above is en route to his fiancée's flat in the Bronx. He has neglected to purchase the customary bouquet for his intended and has offered his seat to the lady, who is standing, in exchange for her corsage bouquet. Should she accept the proposition without further ado, or should she request the guard to introduce the gentleman first?

The young lady has received an invitation to a quilting - bee from a Mrs. Steenwyck and, anxious to make a correct reply, she has bought a Complete Letter Writer to aid her to this end. To her surprise and dismay, she finds that it contains three model replies to such an invitation beginning "Dear Mrs. Peartree," "Dear Mrs. Rombouts," and "Dear Mrs. Bevy," and one invitation to a christening beginning "Dear Mrs. Steenwyck," but no reply to an invitation to a quilting-bee beginning "Dear Mrs. Steenwyck." PERFECT BEHAVIOR *settles such perplexities.*

Crests or other armorial bearings on note-paper are no longer considered absolutely necessary to establish one's social position. Nevertheless, if one feels that note-paper that does not bear the family escutcheon is not quite all that note-paper should be, it is permissible to have it stamped neatly at the top of the first sheet. Care should be exercised to avoid selecting coats-of-arms that might be recognized, such as that of the United States or Great Britain. Rather solicit the taste of a good stationer than commit the blunders depicted above.

amused during the delay. This can be accomplished by any of the conventional methods, such as card tricks, handsprings, and other feats of athletic agility, or making funny jokes about the host who is at work on the tire.

When the damage has been repaired and the car is once more speeding along, leaving behind it mile after mile of dusty road as well as father's best "jack" and set of tire tools, the small boy will suddenly remark, "I'm hungry." His father will then reply, "We'll be at a fine place to eat in ten minutes." Thirty minutes later mother will remark, "Will, that looks like a good place for a picnic over there." The father will reply, "No—we're coming to a wonderful place—just trust me, Mary!" Twenty minutes later Aunt Florence will say, "Will, I think that grove over there would be fine for our lunch," to which the husband will reply, "We're almost at the place I know about—it's ideal for a picnic." Forty minutes after this, father will stop the car and point to a clump of trees. "There,"

[143]

he will say, "what do you think of that?"
"Oh, we can't eat *there!*" will be the answer
of mother, daughter and Aunt Florence.
"Drive on a bit further—I think I know a
place."

Three hours and thirty minutes later (i. e.
four hours past your normal lunch hour) there
will be another puncture and as the car stops
beside a wheat field it will begin to rain, and
the daughter will sigh, "Well, we might as
well eat here." The "picnic" will then be held
in the car, and nothing really quite carries
one back to nature and primeval man as does
warm lemonade and a lettuce sandwich in a
Buick with the top up and side curtains on.

After lunch it will be time to return home,
and after you and father have ruined your
clothes in repairing the punctures, the merry
party will proceed on its way. The next
morning, if you have not caught pneumonia,
you will be able to go to your work greatly re-
freshed by your day's outing in the lap of old
Mother Nature.

BOXING IN AMERICAN SOCIETY

ALTHOUGH many of America's fore-
most boxers have been persons whom one
would not care to know socially, yet much fun
and pleasure can be had out of the "manly
art" if practised in a gentlemanly manner.

"Boxing parties" are generally held in the
evening. The ballroom of one's home can be
pleasantly decorated for the occasion, with a
square ring roped off in the centre surrounded
by seats for the ladies and gentlemen who
come as invited guests. Evening dress is
usually worn.

The contests should be between various
members of one's social "set" who are fond
of the sport and can be counted on to remember at all times that they are gentlemen.

The matches should be arranged in tourna-
ment form, so that the winner of one bout
meets the winner of the next bout, et cetera,
until all but two have been eliminated. The
boxer who wins this final contest shall be
proclaimed the "champion."

[145]

Great fun can then be had by announcing that the "champion" will be permitted to box three rounds with a "masked marvel." The identity of this "unknown" (who is usually Jack Dempsey or some other noted professional pugilist) should be kept carefully secret, so that all the guests are in a glow of mystified excitement when the contest begins, and you can imagine their delight and happy enthusiasm when the "masked marvel" cleverly knocks the "champion" for a double loop through the ropes into the lap of some tittering "dowager."

Refreshments should then be served and the "champion" can be carried home in a car or ambulance provided by the thoughtful host.

BRIDGE WHIST

"BRIDGE whist," or "Bridge," as it is often called by the younger generation, is rapidly replacing whist as the favorite card game of good society, and "bridge" parties are much *en vogue* for both afternoon and evening entertainments. In order to be-

[146]

come an expert "bridge" player one must, of course, spend many months and even years in a study of the game, but any gentleman or lady of average intelligence can, I believe, pick up the fundamentals of "bridge" in a short while.

Let us suppose, for example, that you, as a "young man about town," are invited to play "bridge" on the evening of Friday, November seventeenth, at the home of Mrs. Franklin Gregory. Now, although you may have played the game only once or twice in your life, it would never do to admit the fact, for in good society one is supposed to play "bridge" just as one is supposed to hate newspaper publicity, and on the evening of Friday, November seventeenth, you should present yourself in suitable attire at Mrs. Gregory's home.

There you will find fifteen or twenty other guests, and after a few minutes of light social banter a bell will ring and the players will take their places. At your table will be Mrs. F. Jamison Dollings (your partner) and Mr. and

[147]

Mrs. Theodore Watts. Mrs. Dollings (Sept. 6, 1880) is considered one of the most expert "bridge" players in the city, while Mr. Watts has one of the largest retail clothing stores in the central part of the State. Mrs. Watts was one of the Van Cortlandt girls (the plain one).

As you are probably (next to Mr. and Mrs. Watts) the worst "bridge" player in the room it should be your duty to make up for this deficiency by keeping the other three players conversationally stimulated, for nothing so enlivens a game of "bridge" as a young man or woman with a pleasing personality and a gift for "small talk." Thus, at the very beginning, after you have finished dealing the cards, you should fill in what seems to you an embarrassing pause by telling one of your cleverest stories, at the conclusion of which Mrs. Dollings will remark, "We are waiting for your bid, Mr. S——."

The etiquette of "bidding," as far as you are concerned, should resolve itself into a consistent effort on your part to become "dummy" for each and every game. The minute your partner (Mrs. Dollings) bids anything, it should be your duty as a gentleman to see that she gets it, no matter what the cost.

Thus, on the first hand, you "pass." Mr. Watts then says, "Wait a minute, till I get these cards fixed"; to which Mrs. Watts replies, "Theodore, for Heaven's sake, how long do you want?" Mr. Watts then says, "Which is higher—clubs or hearts?" to which Mrs. Watts replies, "Clubs." Mrs. Dollings then says, "I beg your pardon, but hearts have always been considered higher than clubs." Mrs. Watts says, "Oh, yes, of course," and gives Mr. Watts a mean look. Mr. Watts then says, "I bid—let's see—I bid two spades —no, two diamonds." Mrs. Dollings quickly says, "Two lilies," Mr. Watts says, "What's a lily?" to which Mrs. Watts replies, "Theodore!" and then bids "Two spades," at which Mrs. Dollings says, "I beg your pardon, but I have just bid two spades." Mr. Watts then chuckles, and Mrs. Watts says (but not to Mr. Watts), "I beg your pardon." Mrs.

Watts then bids "Three spades," at which you quickly say, "Four spades."

This bid is not "raised." Mrs. Dollings then says to you, "I am counting on your spades to help me out," at which you look at the only spade in your hand (the three) and answer, "Ha! Ha! Ha!" There is then a wait of four minutes, at the end of which Mrs. Dollings wearily says, "It is your first lead, is it not, Mrs. Watts?" Mrs. Watts then blushes, says, "Oh, I beg your pardon!" and leads the four of hearts. You then lay down your "dummy" hand. Before Mrs. Dollings has had time to discover just what you have done to her, you should rise quickly and say, "Excuse me, but I want to use the telephone a minute." You should then go into the next room and wait ten or fifteen minutes. When you return Mrs. Dollings will have disappeared, Mrs. Watts will be looking fixedly at Mr. Watts, and Mr. Watts will be saying, "Well, it's a silly game, anyway."

You and Mr. and Mrs. Watts can then have

a nice game of twenty-five cent limit stud poker for the rest of the evening, and it would certainly be considered a thoughtful and gracious "gesture" if, during the next two or three weeks, you should call occasionally at the hospital to see how Mrs. Dollings is "getting on," or you might even send some flowers or a nice potted plant.

FORMAL AND INFORMAL DRINKING

"DRINKING" has, of course, always been a popular sport among the members of the better classes of society, but never has the enthusiasm for this pastime been so great in America as since the advent of "prohibition." Gentlemen and ladies who never before cared much for "drinking" have now given up almost all other amusements in favor of this fascinating sport; young men and débutantes have become, in the last few years, fully as expert in the game as their parents. In many cities "drinking" has become more popular than "bridge" or dancing and it is predicted that, with a few more years of "prohibition," "drinking" will supersede golf and baseball as the great American pastime.

The effect of this has been to change radically many of the fundamental rules of the sport, and the influence on the etiquette of the game has been no less marked. What was considered "good form" in this pastime among our forefathers is now decidedly *démodé,* and the correct drinker of 1910 is as obsolete and out of date in the present decade as the "frock-coat."

The game today is divided into (a) formal and (b) informal drinking. "Formal drinking" is usually played after dinner and is more and more coming to take the place of charades, sleight-of-hand performances, magic lantern shows, "dumb crambo," et cetera, as the parlor amusement *par excellence*. "Formal drinking" can be played by from one to fifteen people in a house of ordinary dimensions; for a larger number it is generally better to provide a garage, a large yard, and special police, fire and plate glass insurance. The game is played with glasses, ice, and a dozen bottles of either whisky or gin.

The sport is begun by the host's wife, who says, "How would you all like to play a little bridge?" This is followed by silence. Another wife then says, "I think it would be awfully nice to play a little bridge." One of the men players then steps forward and says, "I think it would be awfully nice to have a little drink."

An "It" is then selected—always, by courtesy, the host. The "It" then says, "How would you all like to have a little drink?" The men players then answer in the affirmative, and the "It's" wife says, "Now, Henry dear, please—remember what happened last time." The "It" replies, "Yes, dear," and goes into the cellar, while the "It's" wife, after providing each guest with a glass, puts away the Dresden china clock, the porcelain parrot, and the gold fish globe.

Sides are chosen—usually with the husbands on one "team" and the wives on the other. The purpose of the game is for the

[153]

"husbands' team" to try to drink up all the "It's" liquor before the "wives' team" can get them to go home.

When the "It" returns with the liquor he pours out a portion for each player and at a given signal all drink steadily for several minutes. The "It's" wife then says, "Now—how about a few rubbers of bridge?" She is immediately elected "team captain" for the rest of the evening. It is the duty of the "team captain" to provide cracked ice and water, to get ready the two spare bedrooms, to hold Wallie Spencer's hand, to keep Eddie Armstrong from putting his lighted cigaret ends on the piano, and to break up the party as soon as possible. The game generally ends when (1) the liquor is all gone, (2) the "It" (or three guests) have passed "out," (3) Wallie Spencer starts telling about his war experiences.

"Informal" drinking needs, of course, no such elaborate preparations and can be played anywhere and any time there is anything to drink. The person who is caught with the liquor is "It," and the object of the game is to take all the liquor away from the "It" as soon as possible. In order to avoid being "It," many players sometimes resort to various low subterfuges, such as sneaking down alone to the club locker-room during a dance, but this practise is generally looked upon with great disfavor—especially by that increasingly large group of citizens who are unselfishly devoting their lives to the cause of a "dry America" by consuming all of the present rapidly diminishing visible supply.

A JOLLY HALLOWE'EN PARTY

THE problem of providing suitable entertainment for one's informal parties is something which has perplexed many a host and hostess in recent years. How often has it happened that just when you had gotten your guests nicely seated around the parlor listening to the Caruso record, some ill-mannered fellow would remark, "Oh, Lord—let's go over to the Tom Phillips' and get something to drink." How many times in the past have you prepared original little "get-together" games, such as Carol Kennicott did in *Main Street,* only to find that, when you again turned the lights on, half the company had disappeared for the evening.

Of course we cannot all be as startlingly clever as Carol, but Hallowe'en, which comes this year on October 31st, offers a splendid opportunity for originality and "peppy" fun. The following suggestions are presented to ambitious hostesses with the absolute guaranty that no matter what other reactions her guests may have, they will certainly not be bored.

INVITATIONS

THE whole spirit of Hallowe'en is, of course, one of "spooky" gayety and light-hearted ghastliness. Witches and ghosts run riot; corpses dance and black cats howl. "More work for the undertaker" should be the leitmotif of the evening's fun.

The moribund spirit can be delightfully observed, first of all, in the preparation of the invitations. I know of one hostess, for instance, who gained a great reputation for originality by enclosing a dead fish with each bidding to the evening's gayeties. It is, of course, not at all necessary to follow her example to the letter; the enclosure of anything dead will suffice, providing, of course, that it is not *too* dead. There is such a thing as carrying a joke beyond the limits of propriety, and the canons of good taste should always be respectfully observed.

Another amusing way of preparing invitations is to cut out colored paper in the shape of cats, witches, etc., upon which appropriate verses are inscribed. Such as:

"Next Monday night is Hallowe'en,
You big stiff."

or

"On Monday next comes All-Hallows-Even,
My grandmother's maiden name was Stephens."

or

"On Hallowe'en you may see a witch
If you don't look out, you funny fellow."

or

"Harry and I are giving a Hallowe'en party;
Harry says you owe him four dollars; please be
prompt."

or

"Monday night the ghosts do dance;
Why didn't you enlist and go to France,
You slacker?"

[157]

Another novel invitation is made by cutting a piece of yellow paper thirteen inches long and four inches wide, and writing on each inch one of the lines given below. Then begin at the bottom and fold the paper up, inch by inch. Fasten the last turn down with a "spooky" gummed sticker, and slip into a small envelope. When the recipient unfolds the invitation, he will be surprised to read the following:

> Now what on earth
> do you suppose
> is in this
> little folder
> keep turning
> ha ha ha
> further
> ha ha ha
> further
> ha ha ha
> further
> ha ha ha
> further

It would perhaps be best to telephone the next day to those guests whom you really want, and give them further details as to the date and time of the party. Additional fun can be

Few people realize the value of picture post-cards as indicators of the birth, breeding, and character of the sender, yet nothing so definitely "places" a person socially as his choice of these souvenirs. Could you have selected the senders of the above cards?

In spite of his haughty airs and fine clothes, the gentleman betrays that he is not much accustomed to good society when, having been asked by his hostess if he would care to remove his coat and waistcoat during the warm evening of bridge, he, in doing so, reveals the presence of several useful cards hidden about his person. This sort of thing, while often tolerated at less formal "stag" poker-parties, is seldom, if ever, permissible when ladies are present. The young man was simply ignorant of the fact that Hoyle and not Herman the Great is the generally accepted authority on cards in the "beau monde."

gotten out of this invitation by failing to put postage stamps on the envelopes when you mail them; the two cents which each guest will have to pay for postage due can be returned in a novel manner on the night of the party by inserting them in sandwiches or stuffed tomatoes.

For those who may wish to send out more elaborate invitations, the following distinctly original plan is suggested: Procure a number of small alarm clocks and a quantity of nitroglycerine or other high explosive. Insert in each clock a small amount of the nitroglycerine, being careful not to put too much; a quantity sufficient to wreck a room 20x30 will generally suffice. Then arrange the alarm mechanism so that the explosion will occur at 12 midnight. Attach to the clock a card, neatly decorated with witches, goblins, etc., on which is written

> "Midnight is the mystic hour
> Of yawning graves and coffins dour.
> Beneath your bed this clock please hide
> And when it strikes—you'll be surprised."

[159]

These clocks should then be delivered in the afternoon to those of the guests whom you are merely inviting because they are your husband's business associates, or because they were nice to your mother when she did her own work. Later on, in order to avoid hard feelings on the part of relatives and friends of the deceased, it might be well to explain to them that you sent the clocks only in the spirit of Hallowe'en fun; it might even help to invite them to one of your next parties.

RECEIVING THE GUESTS

ON Hallowe'en night great care should be taken in the preparations for receiving the guests in a mystic manner; no pains should be spared in the effort to start the evening off with a "bang."

Several novel ideas are offered for starting the guests off on the right informal spirit. Before they arrive, it is a good plan to take the street number off your house and fasten it to the porch of your next door neighbors, who will, of course, be at home because they are

[160]

perfectly impossible people whom no one would invite anywhere. Extinguish all the lights in your own house; your neighbor, as he comes downstairs twenty-five or thirty times in the next hour, will obligingly tell your bewildered friends specifically where to go.

When the guest finally learns from the neighborhood policeman which house on the block is really yours he will discover on your door a sign reading:

> "If you would be my Valentine,
> Follow please the bright green line."

Leading from the door is a green cord which the mystified guest proceeds to follow, according to directions. This cord should guide the way to the coal cellar of your other neighbor who has recently purchased an automatic revolver under the delusion that burglars are operating in the neighborhood. As your bewildered guest gropes his way about the cellar, it is quite likely that he will be shot at several times and by the time he emerges (if he does emerge) he will be quite delightfully full of the informal spirit of Hallowe'en and ready for anything.

HOW TO MYSTIFY

A T this point, your wife, dressed as a witch, should unexpectedly rush out at him; there is always the delightful possibility that he will pick up a convenient rock and brain her on the spot—an event which often adds an unexpected touch of gayety to the evening's fun. If, however, no such event occurs, the guest should be blindfolded and led into the house. Once inside he is conducted upstairs to the attic, where he will find three or four earlier arrivals also blindfolded.

The hands and feet of these four are then securely tied and they are told that they are to be left there all evening. This is really a great joke, because they do not, of course, at the time, believe what you say, and when you come up to untie them the next morning, their shame-faced discomposure is truly laughable.

The green-cord-into-neighbor's-coal-cellar joke can be cleverly varied by taking the lid off your cistern and making the green line lead in that direction. Great care should be taken, however, to keep an exact account of the number of guests who succumb to this trick, for although an unexpected "ducking" is excruciatingly humorous, drowning often results fatally.

Great fun can be added to the evening's entertainment by dressing several of the guests as ghosts, witches, corpses, etc; these costumes can be quite simply and economically made in the home, or can be procured from some reliable department store.

An "old-fashioned" witch's costume consists of a union suit (Munsing or any other standard brand), corset, brassière, chemise, underpetticoat, overpetticoat, long black skirt, long black stockings, shoes, black waist and shawl, with a pointed witch's hat and a broomstick. The "modern" witch's costume is much simpler and inexpensive in many details.

A particularly novel and "hair raising" effect may be produced by painting the entire body of one of the male guests with phos-

[163]

phorus. As this glowing nude stalks uncannily through the darkened rooms you may easily imagine the ghastly effect—especially upon his wife.

GAMES

AFTER the guests have sufficiently amused themselves with the ghosts and witches it will be time to commence some of the many games which are always associated with Hallowe'en.

"Bobbing for apples" is, of course, the most common of these games and great sport it is, too, to watch the awkward efforts of the guests as they try to pick up with their teeth the apples floating in a large tub. I know of one hostess who added greatly to the evening's fun by pouring twelve quarts of gin into the tub; the effect on the bobbers was, of course, extremely comical, except for the unfortunate conduct of two gentlemen, one of whom went to sleep in the tub, the other so far forgetting himself as playfully to throw all the floating fruit at the hostess' pet Pomeranian.

The Etiquette of Games and Sports

Most Hallowe'en games concern themselves with delving into the future in the hopes that one may there discover one's husband or bride-to-be. In one of these games the men stand at one end of the room, facing the girls, with their hands behind their backs and eyes tightly closed. The girls are blindfolded and one by one they are led to within six feet of the expectant men and given a soft pin cushion which they hurl forward. The tradition is that whichever man the girl hits, him will she marry. Great fun can be added to the game by occasionally substituting a rock or iron dumb-bell in place of the romantic pin cushion.

Another game based on a delightful old Hallowe'en tradition is as follows: A girl is given a lighted candle and told to walk upstairs into the room at the end of the hall where, by looking in a mirror, she will see her future husband. Have it arranged so that you are concealed alone in the room. When the girl arrives, look over her shoulder into the mirror. She had better go downstairs after ten minutes, though, so that another girl can come up. This tradition dates from before William the Conqueror.

No Hallowe'en is complete, of course, without fortune telling. Dress yourself as a wizard and have the guests led in one by one to hear their fortune told. Hanging in front of you should be a caldron, from which you extract the slip of paper containing the particular fortune. These slips of paper should be prepared beforehand. The following are suggested:

"You will meet a well dressed, good looking man who understands you better than your husband. How about Thursday at the Plaza?"

"You are about to receive a shipment of Scotch whisky that you ordered last month. And it's about time you kicked across with some of your own."

"You will have much trouble in your life if you lie about your golf score as you did last Sunday on Number 12."

Still another pleasing Hallowe'en game,

based on the revelation of one's matrimonial future, is played as follows: Seven lighted candles are placed in a row on a table. The men are then blindfolded, whirled around three times and commanded to blow out the candles. The number extinguished at a blow tells the number of years before they meet their bride. This game only grows interesting, of course, when some old goat with long whiskers can be induced to take a blind shot at blowing out the candles. Have Pyrene convenient—but not too convenient to spoil the fun.

For the older members of the party, the host should provide various games of cards and dice. In keeping with the ghastly spirit of the occasion, it would be well to have the dice carefully loaded. Many hosts have thus been able to make all expenses and often a handsome profit out of the evening's entertainment.

If the crap game goes particularly well, many hosts do not hesitate to provide elaborate refreshments for the guests. Here, too, the spirit of fun and jollity should prevail, and great merriment is always provoked by the ludicrous expression of the guest who has broken two teeth on the cast-iron olive. Other delightful surprises should be arranged, and a little Sloan's liniment in the punch or ground glass in the ice cream will go a long way toward making the supper amusing. And finally, when the guests are ready to depart and just before they discover that you have cut cute little black cats and witches out of the backs of their evening wraps and overcoats, it would perhaps be well to run upstairs and lock yourself securely in your room.

Chapter Eight

CORRESPONDENCE AND INVITATIONS

CHAPTER EIGHT: CORRESPONDENCE AND INVITATIONS

CORRESPONDENCE

IT is narrated of a well-known English lady (who is noted on the other side of the Atlantic for the sharpness of her wit) that on one occasion, when a vainglorious American was boasting of his country's prowess in digging the Panama Canal, she calmly waited until he had finished and then replied, with an indescribable smile, "Ah—but you Americans do not know how to write letters." Needless to say the discomfited young man took himself off at the earliest opportunity.

There is much truth, alas, in the English lady's clever retort, for the automatic typewriter, the telegraph, and the penny postal card have done much to cause a gradual decline in the gentle art of correspondence. As one American woman recently remarked to a

[171]

visitor (with more wit, however, than good taste), "Yes, we do have correspondents here —but they are all in the divorce courts."

CORRESPONDENCE FOR YOUNG LADIES

THERE are certain rules in regard to correct letter-writing which must be followed by all who would "take their pen in hand." Young people are the most apt to offend in this respect against the accepted canons of good taste and it is to these that I would first address the contents of this chapter. A young girl often lets her high spirits run away with her *amour propre,* with the result that her letters, especially those addressed to strangers, are often lacking in that dignity which is the *sine qua non* of correct correspondence.

Consider, for example, the following two letters composed by Miss Florence ......, a débutante of New York City, who is writing to a taxidermist thanking him for his neat work in having recently stuffed her deceased pet Alice. The first of these letters illustrates the evil to which I have just referred, viz., the

[172]

Correspondence and Invitations

complete absence of proper dignity. The second, written with the aid of her mama, whose experience in social affairs has been considerable, shows the correct method of corresponding with comparative strangers.

An Incorrect Letter from a Débutante to a Taxidermist Thanking Him for Having Stuffed Her Pet Alice

DEAR MR. EPPS:

Aren't you an old *peach* to have gone and stuffed Alice so prettily! Really, Mr. Epps, I never saw such a knockout piece of taxidermy, even in Europe, and I simply adore it. Mother gave a dinner party last night and *everybody* was just wild about it and wanted to know who had done it. How on *earth* did you manage to get the wings to stay like that? And the eyes are just too priceless for words. Honestly, every time I look at it, it's so *darned* natural that I can't believe Alice is really dead. I guess you must be pretty dog-goned crazy about birds yourself to have done such a lovely job on Alice, and I guess you know how perfectly sick I was over her death. Honestly, Mr. Epps, she was *such* a *peach* of an owl. But I suppose it had to be, and anyway, thanks just heaps for having done such a really perfectly gorgeous bit of taxidermy.

Gratefully,
FLORENCE CHASE.

593 Fifth Avenue,
New York City.

[173]

Perfect Behavior

The above is, you observe, quite lacking in that reserve with which young ladies should always treat strange gentlemen and especially those who are not in their own social "set." Slang may be excusable in shop girls or baseball players, but never in the mouth of a young lady with any pretensions to breeding. And the use of "darned" and "dog-goned" is simply unpardonable. Notice, now, the way in which Miss Florence writes the letter after her mama has given her the proper instruction.

A Correct Letter from a Débutante to a Taxidermist Thanking Him for Having Stuffed Her Pet Alice

Mr. Lloyd Epps, Taxidermist,
New York City.
DEAR SIR:
It is with sincere pleasure that I take my pen in hand to compliment you upon the successful manner in which you have rendered your services as taxidermist upon my late owl Alice. Death in the animal kingdom is all too often regarded with an unbecoming levity or, at least, a careless lack of sympathetic appreciation, and it is with genuine feelings of gratitude that I pen these lines upon the occasion of the receipt of the sample of the excellent manner in

The young man is leaving the home of his host in "high dudgeon." He is of the type rather slangily known among the members of our younger set as "finale hopper" which means, in the "King's English," one who is very fond of dancing. His indignation is well founded, since it is not the custom among members of the socially elite to comment in the presence of the guest on either the quantity of soup consumed or the method of consumption adopted. These things should be left for the privacy of the boudoir or smoking den where they will afford much innocent amusement. Nor is the host mending matters by his kindly meant but perhaps tactless offer of a nickel for carfare.

*The gentleman with the excellent teeth has just been
guilty of a gross social error. Wrongly supposing
that the secret of popularity lies in a helpful spirit
and having discovered that the son of his hostess
is about to enter a dental school, he has removed
the excellent teeth (false) from his mouth and passed
them around for inspection. The fact that the
teeth are of the latest mode does not in any way
condone the breach. Leniency in such matters is
not recommended. "Facilis descensus Averni" as
one of the great poets of the Middle Ages so aptly
put it.*

which you have performed your task. Of the same opinion is my father, a vice-president of the Guaranty Trust Co., and himself a taxidermist of no inconsiderable merit, who joins me in expressing to you our most grateful appreciation.

Sincerely yours,

FLORENCE ELIOT CHASE.

December 11, 1922.

COLLEGE BOYS

IT is the tendency of the age to excuse many social errors in young people, and especially is this true of the mischievous pranks of college boys. If Harvard football heroes and their "rooters," for example, wish to let their hair grow long and wear high turtle-necked red "sweaters," corduroy trousers and huge "frat" pins, I, for one, can see no grave objection, for "boys will be boys" and I am, I hope, no "old fogy" in such matters. But I also see no reason why these same young fellows should not be interested in the graces of the salon and the arts of the drawing-room. Consider, for example, the following two letters, illustrating the correct and incorrect method in which two young college men should corre-

[175]

spond, and tell me if there is not some place in our college curriculum for a Professor of Deportment:

An Incorrect Letter from a Princeton Student to a Yale Student Congratulating the Latter on His Football Victory

DEAR MIKE:
Here's your damn money. I was a fool to give you odds.

ED.

P. S. What happened at the Nass? I woke up Sunday with a terrific welt on my forehead and somebody's hat with the initials L. G. T., also a Brooks coat. Do you know whose they are?

P. P. S. Please for God's sake don't cash this check until the fifteenth or I'm ruined.

And here is the way in which I would suggest that this same letter be indited.

A Correct Letter from a Princeton Student to a Yale Student Congratulating the Latter on His Football Victory

MY DEAR "FRIENDLY ENEMY":
Well, well, it was a jolly game, wasn't it, and it was so good to see you in "Old Nassau." I am sorry that you could not have come earlier in the fall,

when the trees were still bronze and gold. I also regret exceedingly that you did not stay over until Sunday, for it would have been such a treat to have taken you to see the Graduate School buildings and the Cleveland Memorial Tower. However, "better luck next time."

The enclosed check is, as you may well guess, in payment of our wager on the result of the gridiron contest. Truly, I am almost glad that I lost, for I can not but think that gambling in any form is at best an unprofitable diversion, and this has taught me, I hope, a lesson from which I may well benefit. Do not think me a "prig," dear Harry, I beg of you, for I am sure that you will agree with me that even a seemingly innocent wager on a football match may lead in later life to a taste for gambling with dice and cards or even worse. Shall we not agree to make this our last wager—or at least, next time, let us not lend it the appearance of professional gambling by giving "odds," such as I gave you this year.

You must have thought it frightfully rude of me not to have seen you to the train after that enjoyable evening at the Nassau Inn, but to tell you the truth, Harry, the nervous excitement of the day proved too much for me and I was forced to retire. My indisposition was further accentuated by a slight mishap which befell me outside the Inn but which need cause you no alarm as a scalp wound was the only result and a few days' rest in my cozy dormitory room will soon set matters to rights. I trust, however, that you will explain to your friends the cause of my sudden departure and my seeming inhospitality. Such jolly fellows they were—and I am only too glad to find that the "bulldogs" are as thoroughly nice as the chaps we have down here. Incidentally, I discovered, somewhat to my dismay, as you may well imagine, that in taking my departure I inadvertently "walked off" with the hat and overcoat of one of your friends whose initials are L. G. T. I am mortified beyond words and shall send the garments to you by the next post with my deepest apologies to the unlucky owner.

Rest assured, Harry my friend, that I am looking forward to visiting you some time in the near future, for I have always been curious to observe the many interesting sights of "Eli land." Particularly anxious am I to see the beautiful trees which have given New Haven its name of "the City of Elms," and the collection of primitive paintings for which your college is justly celebrated. And in closing may I make the slight request that you postpone the cashing of my enclosed check until the fifteenth of this month, as, due to some slight misunderstanding, I find that my account is in the unfortunate condition of being "overdrawn."

Believe me, Harry, with kindest regards to your nice friends and yourself and with congratulations on the well deserved victory of your "eleven,"

Your devoted friend and well wisher,

EDWARD ELLIS COCHRAN.

LETTERS TO PARENTS

OF course, when young people write to the members of their immediate family, it is not necessary that they employ such reserve as in correspondence with friends. The following letter well illustrates the change in tone which is permissible in such intimate correspondence:

A Correct Letter from a Young Lady in Boarding School to Her Parents

DEAR MOTHER:

Of course I am terribly glad that you and father are thinking of coming to visit me here at school next week, but don't you think it would be better if, instead of your coming all the way up here, I should come down and stay with you in New York? The railroad trip up here will be very hard on you, as the trains are usually late and the porters and conductors are notorious for their gruffness and it is awfully hard to get parlor-car seats and you know what sitting in a day-coach means. I should love to have you come only I wouldn't want you or father to get some terrible sickness on the train and last month there were at least three wrecks on that road, with many fatalities, and when you get here the accommodations aren't very good for outsiders, many of the guests having been severely poisoned only last year by eating ripe olives and the beds, they say, are extremely hard. Don't you really think it would be ever so much nicer if you and father stayed in some comfortable hotel in New York with all the conveniences in the world and there are some wonderful things at the theaters which you really ought to see. I could probably get permission from Miss Spencer to come and visit you over Saturday and Sunday if you are stopping at one of the five hotels on her "permitted" list.

However, if you do decide to come here, perhaps

it would be better to leave father in New York because I know he wouldn't like it at all with nothing but women and girls around and I am sure that he couldn't get his glass of hot water in the morning before breakfast and he would have a much better time in New York. But if he does come please mother don't let him wear that old gray hat or that brown suit, and mother couldn't you get him to get some gloves and a cane in New York before he comes? And please, mother dear, make him put those "stogies" of his in an inside pocket and would you mind, mother, not wearing that brooch father's employees gave you last Christmas?

I shall be awfully glad to see you both but as I say it would be better if you let me come to New York where you and father will be ever so much more comfortable.

Your loving daughter,

JEANNETTE.

LETTERS FROM PARENTS

THE same familiarity may be observed by parents when corresponding with their children, with, of course, the addition of a certain amount of dignity commensurate with the fact that they are, as it were, *in loco parentis.* The following example will no doubt be of aid to parents in correctly corresponding with their children:

Correspondence and Invitations

A Correct Letter from a Mother to Her Son Congratulating Him on His Election to the Presidency of the United States

DEAR FREDERICK:

I am very glad that you have been elected President of the United States, Frederick, and I hope that now you will have sense enough to see Dr. Kincaid about your teeth. It would be well to have him give you a thorough looking over at this time. And Mrs. Peasely has given me the name of a splendid throat specialist in New York whom I wish you would see as soon as possible, for it has been almost a year since you went to Dr. Ryan. Are you getting good wholesome food? Mrs. Dennison stopped in this morning and she told me that Washington is very damp in the spring and I think you had better get a new overcoat—a heavy warm one. She also told me the name of a place where you can buy real woolen socks and pajamas. I hope that you aren't going to be so foolish as to wear those short B. V. D.'s all winter because now that you are president you must take care of yourself, Edward dear. Are you keeping up those exercises in the morning? I found those dumb-bells of yours in the attic yesterday and will send them on to you if you wish. And, dear, please keep your throat covered when you go out— Mrs. Kennedy says that the subways are always cold and full of draughts. I saw a picture of you at the "movies" the other evening and you were making a speech in the rain without a hat or rubbers. Your uncle Frederick was just such a fool as you are about wearing rubbers and he almost died of pneumonia the winter we moved to Jefferson Avenue. Be sure and let me know what Dr. Kincaid says and tell him *everything*.

Your *loving* mother.

P. S. What direction does your window face?

LETTERS TO PROSPECTIVE FATHERS-IN-LAW

A YOUNG man desiring to marry a young girl does not, in polite society, "pop the question" to her by mail, unless she happens, at the time, to be out of the city or otherwise unable to "receive." It is often advisable, however, after she has said "yes," to write a letter to her father instead of calling on him to ask for his permission to the match, as a personal interview is often apt to result unsatisfactorily. In writing these letters to prospective fathers-in-law, the cardinal point is, of course, the creation by the young man of a good impression in the mind of the father, and for this purpose he should study to make his letter one which will appeal irresistibly to the older gentleman's habits and tastes.

Thus, in writing to a father who is above everything else a "business man," the following form is suggested:

[182]

Correspondence and Invitations

A Correct Letter to a Prospective Father-in-Law Who Is a Business Man

My letter,
10-6-22
Your letter,

In reply please refer to: ———

File—Love—personal—N. Y.—1922
No. G, 16 19

Mr. Harrison Williams,
Vice-Pres. Kinnear-Williams Mfg. Co.,
Buffalo, N. Y.

DEAR SIR:
Confirming verbal message of even date re: being in love with your daughter, this is to advise that I am in love with your daughter. Any favorable action which you would care to take in this matter would be greatly appreciated.

Yours truly,
EDWARD FISH.

Copy to your Daughter   per E. F.
  "   "   " Wife
EF/F

Or, should the girl's father be prominent in the advertising business, the following would probably create a favorable impression, especially if printed on a blotter or other useful article:

Perfect Behavior

A Correct Letter to a Prospective Father-in-Law Who Is in the Advertising Business

JUST A MOMENT!

Have you ever stopped to consider the problem of grandchildren?

Do you know, for example, that ONLY 58% of the fathers in America are GRANDFATHERS?

Did it ever occur to you that only 39% of the grandfathers in America EVER HAVE GRANDCHILDREN?

Honestly, now, don't there come moments, after the day's work is done and you are sitting in your slippers before the fire, when you would give anything in the world for a soft little voice to call you GRANDPA?

Be fair to your daughter
Give her a College educated husband!
COMPLIMENTS OF EDWARD FISH

Perhaps, if the old gentleman is employed in the Credit Department of Brooks Brothers, Frank Brothers, or any one of the better class stores, the following might prove effective:

A Correct Letter to a Prospective Father-in-Law Who Is Employed in a Credit Department

My dear Mr. Roberts: 10-6-22

I am writing you in regard to a little matter of matrimony which no doubt you have overlooked in

[184]

the press of business elsewhere. This is not to be considered as a "dun" but merely as a gentle reminder of the fact that it would be extremely agreeable if you could see fit to let me marry your daughter before the first of next month. I feel sure that you will give this matter your immediate attention.

Yours truly,

Ed. Fish.

11-2-22

Dear Mr. Roberts:

As you have not as yet replied to my communication of 10-6-22 regarding marriage to your daughter, I presume that you were not at the time disposed to take care of the matter to which I referred. I feel sure that upon consideration you will agree that my terms are exceedingly liberal and I must therefore request that you let me have some word from you before the first of next month.

Yours truly,

Edward Fish.

(Registered Mail)   12-2-22

Dear Sir:

You have not as yet replied to my communication of 10-6-22 and 11-2-22. I should regret exceedingly being forced to place this matter in the hands of my attorneys, Messrs. Goldstein and Nusselmann, 41 City Nat'l Bank Bldg.

E. Fish.

Of course, it would never do to carry this series to its conclusion and if no reply is received to this last letter it might be well to call on the gentleman in his place of business—or, possibly, it might even be better to call off the engagement. "None but the brave deserve the fair"—but there is also a line in one of Byron's poems which goes, I believe, "Here sleep the brave."

LOVE LETTERS

A YOUNG man corresponding with his fiancée is never, of course, as formal as in his letters to other people. This does not mean, however, that his correspondence should be full of silly meaningless "nothings." On the contrary, he should aim to instruct and benefit his future spouse as well as convey to her his tokens of affection. The following letter well illustrates the manner in which a young man may write his fiancée a letter which, while it is replete with proper expressions of amatory good will, yet manages to embody a fund of sensible and useful information:

[186]

Correspondence and Invitations

A Correct Letter from a Young Man Traveling in Europe to His Fiancée

MY DEAREST EDITH:

How I long to see you—to hold tight your hand—to look into your eyes. But alas! you are in Toledo and I am in Paris, which, as you know, is situated on the Seine River near the middle of the so-called Paris basin at a height above sea-level varying from 85 feet to 419 feet and extending 7½ miles from W. to E. and 5½ miles from N. to S. But, dearest, I carry your image with me in my heart wherever I go in this vast city with its population (1921) of 2,856,986 and its average mean rainfall of 2.6 inches, and I wish—oh, how I wish—that you might be here with me. Yesterday, for example, I went to the Père Lachaise cemetery which is the largest (106 acres) and most fashionable cemetery in Paris, its 90,148 (est.) tombs forming a veritable open-air sculpture gallery. And what do you think I found there which made me think of you more than ever? Not the tombs of La Fontaine (d. 1695) and Molière (d. 1673) whose remains, transferred to this cemetery in 1804, constituted the first interments—not the last resting place of Rosa Bonheur (d. 1899) or the victims of the Opéra Comique fire (1887)—no, dearest, it was the tomb of Abelard and Heloïse, those late 11th early 12th century lovers, and you may well imagine what thoughts, centering upon a young lady whose first name begins with E, filled my heart as I gazed at this impressive tomb, the canopy of which is composed of sculptured fragments collected by Lenoir from the Abbey of Nogent-sur-Seine (Aube).

Edith dearest, I am sitting in my room gazing

[187]

first at your dear picture and then out of my window at the Eiffel Tower which is the tallest structure in the world, being 984 feet high (Woolworth Building 750 feet, Washington Obelisk 555 feet, Great Pyramid 450 feet). And although it may sound too romantic, yet it seems to me, dearest, that our love is as strong and as sturdy as this masterpiece of engineering construction which weighs 7,000 tons, being composed of 12,000 pieces of metal fastened by 2,500,000 iron rivets.

Farewell, my dearest one—I must go now to visit the Catacombs, a huge charnelhouse which is said to contain the remains of nearly three million persons, consisting of a labyrinth of galleries lined with bones and rows of skulls through which visitors are escorted on the first and third Saturday of each month at 2 P. M. I long to hold you in my arms.

Devotedly,
PAUL.

CORRESPONDENCE OF PUBLIC OFFICIALS

CONGRESSMEN and other public officials are as a rule more careful correspondents than are men whose letters are never to be seen by the public at large. There is a certain well-defined form for a letter meant for public consumption which distinguishes it from correspondence of a more private nature. Thus a Congressman, writing a "public letter," would cast it in the following form:

[188]

Correspondence and Invitations

A Correct "Public Letter" from a Congressman

Mr. Ellison Lothrop,
Vice-Pres. Washington Co. "Better Citizenship"
League,

MY DEAR MR. LOTHROP:

You have requested that I give to the Washington County Better Citizenship League, of which you are an active vice-president, some expression of my views upon the question of Prohibition.

Sir, can there be any doubt as to the belief of every right thinking American citizen in this matter? The Eighteenth Amendment is here and here, thank God, to stay! The great benefit which Prohibition has done to the poor and the working classes is reason enough for its continued existence. It is for the manufacturers, the professional class, the capitalists to give up gladly whatever small pleasure they may have derived from the use of alcohol, in order that John Jones, workingman, may have money in the bank and a happy home, instead of his Saturday night debauch. In every democracy the few sacrifice for the many—"the greatest good of the greatest number" is the slogan. And I, for one, am proud to have been a member of that legislative body which passed so truly God-bidden and democratic an act as the Eighteenth Amendment.

I beg to remain, with best wishes to your great organization,

Sincerely yours,
WALTER G. TOWNSLEY.

[189]

Perfect Behavior

A Correct Private Letter of a Congressman

DEAR BOB:
Tell that fellow on Mulberry Street that I will pay $135 a case for Scotch and $90 for gin *delivered* and not a cent more.

W. G. T.

LETTERS TO NEWSPAPERS, MAGAZINES, ETC.

ANOTHER type of public correspondence is the letter which is intended for publication in some periodical. This is usually written by elderly gentlemen with whiskers and should be cast in the following form:

A Correct Letter from an Elderly Gentleman to the Editor of a Newspaper or Magazine

To the Editor:
SIR:
On February next, *Deo volente,* I shall have been a constant reader of your worthy publication for forty-one years. I feel, sir, that that record gives me the right *ipso facto* to offer my humble criticism of a statement made in your November number by that worthy critic of the drama, Mr. Heywood Broun. *Humanum est errare,* and I am sure that Mr. Broun (with whom I have unfortunately not the honour of an acquaintance) will forgive me for calling his attention to what is indeed a serious, and I might say, unbelievable, misstatement.

The problem of an introduction when there is no
mutual acquaintance is sometimes perplexing. But
the young man, having had the good taste to purchase a copy of PERFECT BEHAVIOR, is having no
difficulty. He has fastened a rope across the sidewalk in front of the lady's house and, with the aid
of a match and some kerosene, has set fire to the
house. Driven by the heat, the young lady will
eventually emerge and in her haste will fall over
the rope. To a gentleman of gallantry and ingenuity
the rest should be comparatively simple.

A knowledge of the language of flowers is essential
to a successful courtship and may avoid much
unnecessary pain. With the best intentions in the
world the young man is about to present the young
lady with a flower of whose meaning he is in total
ignorance. The young lady, being a faithful student
of PERFECT BEHAVIOR, knows its exact meaning
and it will be perfectly correct for her to turn and,
with a frigid bow, break the pot over the young
man's head. Alas, how differently this romance
might have ended if the so-called "friends" of the
young man had tactfully but firmly pointed out to
him the value of a book on etiquette such as PERFECT
BEHAVIOR.

Correspondence and Invitations

In my younger days, now long past, it was not considered *infra dig* for a critic to reply to such letters as this, and I hope that Mr. Broun will deem this epistle worthy of consideration, and recognize the justice of my complaint.

I remember well a controversy that raged between critic and public for many weeks in the days when Joe Jefferson was playing Rip Van Winkle. Ah, sir, do you remember (but, of course, you don't) that entrance of Joe in the first act with his dog Schneider? That was not my first play by many years, but I believe that it is still my favorite. I think the first time I ever attended a dramatic performance was in the winter of '68 when I was a student at Harvard College. Five of us freshmen went into the old Boston Museum to see *Our American Cousin.* Joe Chappell was with us that night and the two Dawes boys and, I think, Elmer Mitchell. One of the Dawes twins was, I believe, afterwards prominent in the Hayes administration. There were many men besides Will Dawes in that Harvard class who were heard from in later years. Ed Twitchell for one, and "Sam" Caldwell, who was one of the nominees for vice president in '92. I sat next to Sam in "Bull" Warren's Greek class. *There* was one of the finest scholars this country has ever produced—a stern taskmaster, and a thorough gentleman. It would be well for this younger generation if they could spend a few hours in that old classroom, with "Bull" pacing up and down the aisle and all of us trembling in our shoes. But *Delenda est Carthago—fuit Ilium—Requiescat in pace.* I last saw "Bull" at our fifteenth reunion and we were all just as afraid of him as in the old days at Hollis.

But I digress. *Tempus fugit,—*which reminds me of a story "Billy" Hallowell once told at a meeting of the American Bar Association in Minneapolis, in 1906. Hallowell was perhaps the most brilliant after-dinner

[191]

Perfect Behavior

speaker I have ever heard—with the possible exception of **W. D. Evarts.** I shall never forget the speech that Evarts made during the second Blaine campaign.

But I digress. Your critic, Mr. Heywood Broun, says on page 33 of the November issue of your worthy magazine that *The Easiest Way* is the father of all modern American tragedy. Sir, does Mr. Broun forget that there once lived a man named William Shakespeare? Is it possible to overlook such immortal tragedies as *Hamlet* and *Othello?* I think not. *Fiat justitia, ruat cœlum.*

Sincerely,
SHERWIN G. COLLINS.

A Correct Letter from an Indignant Father to an Editor of Low Ideals

To the Editor: Sir:

I have a son—a little fourteen-year-old boy who proudly bears my name. This lad I have brought up with the greatest care. I have spared no pains to make him an upright, moral, God-fearing youth.

I had succeeded, I thought, in inculcating in him all those worthy principles for which our Puritan fathers fought and—aye—died. I do not believe that there existed in our neighborhood a more virtuous, more righteous boy.

From his earliest childhood until now Mrs. Pringle and I have kept him carefully free from any suggestion of evil. We have put in his hands only the best and purest of books; we have not allowed him to attend any motion picture performances other than the yearly visit of the Burton Holmes travelogues, and, last year, a film called *Snow White and Rose Red;* we have forbidden

[192]

him to enter a theater. Roland (for that is his name) has never in his life exhibited any interest in what is known as sex.

Sir, you may imagine my chagrin when my Roland—my boy who, for fourteen years, I have carefully shielded from sin—rushed in last night to where Mrs. Pringle and I were enjoying our evening game of Bézique, bearing in his hand a copy of your magazine which, I presume, he had picked up at some so-called friend's house. "Papa, look," said my boy to me, pointing to the cover of the magazine. "What are these?"

Sir, I looked. Mrs. Pringle gave a shriek, and well may she have. My boy was pointing to a cover on which was what is called—in barroom parlance—a "nude." And not *one* nude but *twelve!*

Sir, you have destroyed the parental labors of fourteen years. I trust you are satisfied.

Yours, etc.,
EVERETT G. PRINGLE.

A Letter from a Member of the Lower Classes. Particular pains should be taken in answering such letters as it should always be our aim to lend a hand to those aspiring toward better things.

To the Editor:
Dear Sir:

I am a motorman on the Third Ave. South Ferry local, and the other day one of the passengers left a copy of your magazine on my car and I want to ask you something which maybe you can tell me and anyway it don't

do no harm to ask what I want to know is will it be O. K.
to wear a white vest with a dinner coat this coming
winter and what color socks I enclose stamps for reply.

Yrs.

ED. WALSH.

*A Correct Letter to the Lost and Found De-
partment of a Periodical, inquiring for a
Missing Relative. This should be referred
to the persons mentioned in the letter who will
probably take prompt and vigorous action.*

Literary Editors:
Dear Sirs:

I have been very much interested in the clever work
of Nancy and Ernest Boyd which has been appearing in
your magazine, and I wonder if you could take the time
to give me a little piece of information about them. You
see there was a Nancy Boyd (her mother was Nancy
Kroomen of Beaver Dam) and her bro. Ernest, who
was neighbors to us for several years, and when they
moved I sort of lost track of them. You know how those
things are. But it's a small world after all, isn't it? and
I shouldn't be at all surprised if this was the same party
and, if it is, will you say hello to Nancy for me, and tell
Ernest that Ed. Gold still comes down from Akron to
see E. W. every Saturday. He'll know who I mean.

Ever sincerely,

MAY WINTERS.

[194]

Correspondence and Invitations

LETTERS TO STRANGERS

IN writing to a person with whom you have only a slight acquaintance, it is a sign of proper breeding to attempt to show the stranger that you are interested in the things in which he is interested. Thus, for example, if you were to write a letter to a Frenchman who was visiting your city for the first time, you would endeavor, as in the following example, to speak to him in his own idiom and put him at his ease by referring to the things with which he is undoubtedly familiar. It is only a "boor" who seeks to impose his own hobbies and interests upon a stranger, disregarding entirely the presumable likes and dislikes of the latter.

A Correct Letter to a French Visitor

Monsieur Jules La Chaise,
Hotel Enterprise,
City.

MONSIEUR:
I hope that you have had a *bon voyage* on your trip from *la belle France,* and my wife and I are looking forward to welcoming you to our city. Al-

though I cannot say, as your great king Louis XV.
so justly remarked, *"L'etat, c'est moi,"* yet I believe
that I can entertain you *comme il faut* during your
stay here. But all *bon mots* aside, would you care to
join us this afternoon in a ride around the city? If
you say the word, *voila!* we shall be at your hotel in
our automobile and I think that you will find here
much that is interesting to a native of Lafayette's
great country and especially to a citizen of Paris.
Did you know, for example, that this city manufac-
tures 38% of the toilet soap and perfumery *je ne sais
quoi* which are used in this state? Of course, our
sewers are not to be compared to yours, *mon Dieu,*
but we have recently completed a pumping station
on the outskirts of the city which I think might almost be denominated an *objet d'art.*

I am enclosing a visitor's card to the City Club
h   , which I wish you would use during your stay.
I am sure that you will find there several *bon vivants*
who will be glad to join you in a game of *vingt et un,*
and in the large room on the second floor is a victrola
with splendid instrumental and vocal records of
"La Marseillaise."

Au revoir until I see you this afternoon.

Robert C. Crocker.

A ND above all, in writing to strangers or
comparative strangers, seek to avoid
the mention of subjects which might be dis-
tasteful to the recipient of the letter. Many a
friendship has been utterly ruined because one
of the parties, in her correspondence or con-

[196]

versation, carelessly referred to some matter—
perhaps some physical peculiarity—upon
which the other was extremely sensitive. The
following letter well illustrates how the use of
a little tact may go "a long way."

A Correct Letter to a Bearded Lady

My dear Mrs. Lenox:

I wonder if you would care to go with us to the opera Wednesday evening? The Cromwells have offered us their box for that night, which accounts for our selection of that particular evening. "Beggars cannot be choosers," and while personally we would all rather go on some other night, yet it is perhaps best that we do not refuse the Cromwells' generous offer. Then, too, Wednesday is really the only evening that my husband and I are free to go, for the children take so much of our time on other nights. I do hope, therefore, that you can go with us Wednesday to hear "The Barber of Seville."

Sincerely,

Esther G. (Mrs. Thomas D.) Franklin.

INVITATIONS

THE form of the invitation depends a great deal upon the character of the function to which one wishes to invite the guests to whom one issues the invitation. Or, to put it more simply, invitations differ according to the nature of the party to which one invites the guests. In other words, when issuing invitations to invited guests one must have due regard for the fact that these invitations vary with the various types of entertainments for which one issues the invitations. That is to say, one would obviously not send out the same form of invitation to a wedding as to a dinner party, and vice versa. This is an iron-clad rule in polite society.

For example, a gentleman and lady named Mr. and Mrs. Weems, respectively, living at 1063 Railroad Ave., wishing to invite a gentleman named Mr. Cleek to dinner, would send him the following engraved invitation:

Mr. and Mrs. Lionel Thong Weems

request the pleasure of

Mr. Wallace Tilford Cleek's

company at dinner

on Tuesday January the tenth

at half after seven o'clock

1063 Railroad Avenue.

[198]

Correspondence and Invitations

This invitation would of course be worded differently for different circumstances, such as, for example, if the name of the people giving the party wasn't Weems or if they didn't live at 1063 Railroad Ave., or if they didn't have any intention of giving a dinner party on that particular evening.

Many prospective hostesses prefer to send written notes instead of the engraved invitation, especially if the dinner is to be fairly informal. This sort of invitation should, however, be extremely simple. I think that most well-informed hostesses would agree that the following is too verbose:

DEAR MR. BURPEE:

    It would give us great pleasure if you would dine with us on Monday next at seven-thirty. By the way, did you know that Mr. Sheldon died yesterday of pneumonia?

                Cordially,
                ESTELLE G. BESSERABO.

For receptions in honor of noted guests, word the invitation in this manner:

[199]

MR. AND MRS. CORNELIUS VANDERBILT
request the pleasure of your company
on Friday evening February sixth
from nine to twelve
AT DELMONICO'S
to meet Asst. Fire-Chief CHARLEY SCHMIDT and
Mrs. SCHMIDT

Invitations to graduating exercises are worded thus:

THE SENIOR CLASS
of the
SOUTH ROCHESTER FEMALE DENTAL INSTITUTE
requests the honor of your presence at the
Commencement Exercises
on Tuesday evening, June the fifth
at eight o'clock
MASONIC OPERA HOUSE
"That Six" Orchestra.

ACCEPTANCES AND REGRETS

RESPONSES to invitations usually take the form of "acceptances" or "regrets." It is never correct, for example, to write the following sort of note:

[200]

Correspondence and Invitations

DEAR MRS. CRONICK:

Your invitation for the 12th inst. received and in reply would advise that I am not at the present time in a position to signify whether or not I can accept. Could you at your convenience furnish me with additional particulars re the proposed affair—number of guests, character of refreshments, size of orchestra, etc.? Awaiting an early reply, I am,

Yours truly,

ALFRED CASS NAPE.

If one wishes to attend the party, one "accepts" on a clean sheet of note-paper with black ink from a "fountain" pen or inkwell. A hostess should not, however, make the mistake of thinking that a large number of "acceptances" implies that anybody really wishes to attend her party.

The following is a standard form of acceptance:

Dr. Tanner accepts with pleasure the kind invitation of Mrs. Frederick Cummings Bussey for Thursday evening, December twelfth, at half after eight.

This note need not be signed. The following "acceptance" is decidedly demode:

DEAR MRS. ASTOR:

Will I be at your ball? Say, can a duck swim? Count on me sure.   FRED.

It is also incorrect and somewhat boorish to write "accepted" across the face of the invitation and return it signed to the hostess.

If one does not care to attend the party, one often sends one's "regrets" although one just as often sends one's "acceptances," depending largely upon the social position of one's hostess. The proper form of "regret" is generally as follows:

Alice Ben Bolt regrets that she will be unable to accept the kind invitation of Major General and Mrs. Hannafield for Wednesday evening at half after eight.

Sometimes it is better to explain in some manner the cause of the "regret," as for example:

Alice Ben Bolt regrets that, owing to an ulcerated tooth in the left side of her mouth, and severe neuralgic pains all up and down her left side, she will be unable to accept the kind invitation of Major General and Mrs. Hannafield for Wednesday evening at half after eight, at "The Bananas."

This is not, however, always necessary.

Chapter Nine

THE ETIQUETTE OF DINNERS AND BALLS

CHAPTER NINE: THE ETIQUETTE OF DINNERS AND BALLS

FORMAL DINNERS IN AMERICA

EATING is an extremely old custom and has been practiced by the better classes of society almost without interruption from earliest times. And "society," like the potentate of the parable whose touch transformed every object into gold, has embellished and adorned the all-too-common habit of eating, until there has been evolved throughout the ages that most charming and exquisite product of human culture—the formal dinner party. The gentleman of today who delightedly dons his dress suit and escorts into a ten-course dinner some lady mountain climber or other celebrity, is probably little aware of what he owes to his forefathers for having so painstakingly devised for him such a pleasant method of spending his time.

But "before one runs, one must learn to

walk"—and the joys of the dinner-party are not to be partaken of without a long preliminary course of training, as many a young man has learned to his sorrow when he discovered that his inelegant use of knife and fork was causing humorous comment up and down the "board" and was drawing upon himself the haughty glances of an outraged hostess. The first requisite of success in dining out is the possession of a complete set of correct table manners—and these, like anything worth while, can be achieved only by patient study and daily practise.

TABLE MANNERS FOR CHILDREN

AS a matter of fact, it is never too early to begin to acquire the technique of correct eating, and the nursery is the best possible place for the first lessons in dining-room behavior. Children should be taught at an early age the fundamentals of "table" manners in such a way that by the time they have reached the years of manhood the correct use of knife, fork, spoon and fingerbowl is to them almost

This is an admirable picture with which to test the
"kiddies'" knowledge of good manners at a dinner
table. It will also keep them occupied as a puzzle
picture since the "faux pas" illustrated herewith
will probably not be apparent to the little ones except
after careful examination. If, however, they have
been conscientiously trained it will not be long
before the brighter ones discover that the spoon has
been incorrectly left standing in the cup, that the
coffee is being served from the right instead of the
left side, and that the lettering of the motto on the
wall too nearly resembles the German style to be
quite "au fait" in the home of any red-blooded
American citizen.

Dessert has been reached and the gentleman in the picture is perspiring freely—in itself a deplorable breach of etiquette. He has been attempting all evening to engage the ladies on either side of him in conversation on babies, Camp's Reducing Exercises, politics, Camp's Developing Exercises, music or Charlie Chaplin, only to be rebuffed by a haughty chin on the one hand and a cold shoulder on the other. If he had taken the precaution to consult Stewart's Lightning Calculator of Dinner Table Conversation (one of the many aids to social success to be found in PERFECT BEHAVIOR) *he would have realized the bad taste characterizing his choice of topics and would not have made himself a marked figure at this well-appointed dinner table.*

second nature. But the parents should remember, above everything else, to instruct their children in such a way that the pupil takes pleasure in his lessons. This is the method which is employed today in every successful school or "kindergarten"; this is the method which really produces satisfactory results.

Thus, for example, if you are a father and your boy Edward persists in bringing his pet tadpole to the table in a glass jar, you should not punish or scold him; a much more effective and graphic method of correcting this habit would be for you to suddenly pick up the tadpole one day at luncheon and swallow it. No whipping or scolding would so impress upon the growing boy the importance of the fact that the dinner table is not the place for pets.

Another effective way of teaching table manners to children consists in making up attractive games about the various lessons to be learned. Thus, whenever you have guests for dinner, the children can play "Boner" which

consists in watching the visitor closely all during the meal in order to catch him in any
irregularity in table etiquette. As soon as the
guest has committed a mistake, the first child
to discover it points his finger at him and
shouts, "Pulled a Boner, Pulled a Boner!"
and the boy or girl who discovers the greatest
number of "Boners" 'during the evening is re-
warded with a prize, based on the following
table of points:

> If the guest has dirty hands, 5 points.
> If the guest uses wrong fork or spoon, 5 points.
> If the guest chokes on bone, 8 points.
> If the guest blows on soup, 5 points.
> If the guest drops fork or spoon, 3 points.
> If the guest spills soup on table, 10 points.
> If the guest spills soup on self, 1 point. ᐧ

Of course it is often well to tell the guests
about the game in advance in order that they
may not feel embarrassed but will enter thoroughly into the spirit of this helpful sport.

A CHILD'S GARDEN OF ETIQUETTE

CHILDREN can also acquire knowledge
more easily if it is imparted to them in
the form of verse or easy rhymes, and many

The Etiquette of Dinners and Balls

valuable facts about the dinner table can be
embodied in children's verses. A few of these
which I can remember from my own happy
childhood are as follows:

Oh, wouldn't it be jolly
To be a nice *hors d'œuvre*
And just bring joy to people
Whom fondest you were of.

Soup is eaten with a spoon
But not to any haunting tune.

Oysters live down in the sea
In zones both temp. and torrid,
And when they are good they are very good
   indeed,
And when they are bad they are horrid.

My papa makes a lovely Bronx
With gin so rare and old,
And two of them will set you right
But four will knock you cold.

The boys with Polly will not frolic
Because she's eaten too much garlic.
Mama said the other day,
"A little goes a long, long way."

A wind came up out of the sea
And said, "Those clams are not for me."

Perfect Behavior

Uncle Frank choked on a bone
From eating shad *au gratin*
Aunt Ethel said it served him right
And went back to her flat in
    NEWARK (spoken)
    Poor Uncle Frank! (chanted)

I love my little finger bowl
So full of late filet of sole.

Cousin George at lunch one day
Remarked, "That apple looks quite tasty."
Now George a dentist's bill must pay
Because he was so very hasty.
The proverb's teachings we must hold
"All that glitters is not gold."
And mama said to George, "Oh, shoot,
You've gone and ruined my glass fruit."

Jim broke bread into his soup,
Jim knocked Mrs. Vanderbilt for a loop.
Kate drank from her finger bowl,
Kate knocked Mrs. Vanderbilt for a goal.
Children who perform such tricks
Are socially in Class G-6.

ETIQUETTE IN THE SCHOOL

OF course, as the children become older, the instruction should gradually come to embrace all forms of correct behaviour, and the youthful games and rhymes should give way to the more complex and intricate problems of mature social etiquette. It is suggested that the teachings during this period may be successfully combined with the young gentleman's or lady's other schoolroom studies; in the case of mathematics, for example, the instruction might be handled in somewhat the following manner:

A Problem in Mathematics (7th grade)

A swimmer starts across a stream which is 450 yards wide. He swims for five minutes at the rate of three miles per hour, and for three minutes at the rate of four miles per hour. He then reaches the other bank, where he sees a young lady five feet ten inches tall, walking around a tree, in a circle the circumference of which is forty-two yards.

   A.   What is the diameter of the circle?
   B.   How fast is the current flowing in the stream?
   C.   At what point would the swimmer land if there were no current in the stream?

Perfect Behavior

D. *At what point does the swimmer actually land?*

E. *But suppose that he has no bathing suit on?*

And so, when the young person has reached the age for his first formal dinner party, he will undoubtedly be able to handle the fundamentals of correct etiquette in a satisfactory manner. But, as in every sport or profession, there are certain refinements—certain niceties which come only after long experience—and it is with a view of helping the ambitious diner-out to master these more complex details, that I suggest that he study carefully the following "unwritten laws" which govern every dinner party.

In the first place, a guest is supposed tacitly to consent to the menu which the hostess has arranged, and the diner-out who makes a habit of saying "Squab, you know, never agrees with me—I wonder if I might have a couple of poached eggs," is apt to find that such squeamishness does not pay in the long run.

Practical jokes are never countenanced at a formal affair of this sort. I do not mean that a certain amount of good-natured fun is out of place, but such "stunts" as pulling the hostess' chair out from under her—or gleefully kicking the shins of your neighbor under the table and shouting "Guess who?"—are decidedly among the "non-ests" of correct modern dinner-table behaviour.

Then, too, it is now distinctly bad form to practise legerdemain or feats of sleight-of-hand at a dinner party. Time was when it was considered correct for a young man who could do card or other tricks to add to the gayety of the party by displaying his skill, but that time is past, and the guest of today, who thinks to make a "hit" by pulling a live rabbit or a potted plant from the back of the mystified hostess or one of the butlers, is in reality only making a "fool" of himself if he only knew it.

The same "taboo" also holds good as concerns feats of juggling and no hostess of today will, I am sure, ever issue a second invitation to a young man who has attempted to enliven her evening by balancing, on his nose, a knife, a radish, a plate of soup and a lighted candle. "Cleverness" is a valuable asset but only up to a certain point, and I know of one unfortunately "clever" young chap who almost completely ruined a promising social career by the unexpected failure of one of his pet juggling tricks and the consequent dumping of a large dish of mashed potatoes on the head of a vice-president of the Equitable Trust Company. Besides, people almost always distrust "clever" persons.

It does not "do," either, to "ride your hobby" at a dinner party, and the real truth as to the cause of the sudden social ostracism of young Freddie H——, a New York clubman of some years ago (now happily deceased), is that on one occasion this young fellow, who had developed a craze for marksmanship amounting almost to a mania, very nearly ruined a dinner party given by a prominent Boston society matron by attempting to shoot the whiskers off a certain elderly gentleman, who happened to be a direct descendant of John Smith and Priscilla Alden.

It might also be remarked that the possession of certain physical gifts—such as the ability to wriggle one's ears or do the "splits"—is in itself no "open sesame" to lasting social success. "Slow and sure" is a good rule for the young man to follow, and although he may somewhat enviously watch his more brilliant colleagues as they gain momentary applause by their ability to throw their thumbs out of joint or squirt water through a hole in their front teeth, yet he may console himself with the thought that "the race is not always to the swift" and that "Rome was not built in a day." The gifts of this world have been distributed fairly equally, and you may be sure that the young girl who has been born a ventriloquist very likely is totally unable to spell difficult words correctly or carry even a simple tune.

Ventriloquism, by the way, is also passing out as a form of dinner party diversion, and it is no longer considered a priceless accomplishment to be able to make a dog bark or a baby cry under the hostess's chair.

CONVERSATION AT DINNER

GRADUALLY, however, conversation— real conversation—is coming into its own as the favorite pastime of dinner guests, and the young man or lady who can keep the conversational "ball" rolling is coming more and more into demand. Good conversationalists are, I fear, born and not made—but by study and practise any ambitious young man can probably acquire the technique, and, with time, mould himself into the kind of person upon whom hostesses depend for the success of their party. As an aid in this direction I have prepared the following chart which I would advise all my readers to cut out and paste in some convenient place so that at their next dinner party it can be readily consulted.

The Etiquette of Dinners and Balls

THIS chart divides the dinner into its various courses, and under each course is given what I call an "opening sentence," together with your partner's probable reply and the topic which is then introduced for discussion. And, most valuable of all, under each such topic I have listed certain helpful facts which will enable you to prolong the conversation along those lines until the arrival of the next course, and the consequent opening of another field for discussion. The chart follows:

I. *Cocktails.*

You say to the partner on your right: "What terrible gin!" She (he) replies: "Perfectly ghastly." This leads to a discussion of: Some Aspects of Alcohol. Helpful Facts:

1. An oyster soaked in alcohol becomes quite rigid in eleven minutes.

[217]

2. Senator Volstead was born Sept. 4, 1869.

3. Alcohol, if taken in too great quantities, often produces internal disorders.

II. *Oysters.*

You say to the partner on your right: "Think of being an oyster!"

She (he) replies: "How perfectly ghastly."

This leads to a discussion of: Home Life of Oysters.

Helpful Facts:

1. The average life of an oyster is 38 days, 11 hours.

2. Polygamy is practised among certain classes of oysters.

3. The first oyster was eaten by Ossip Gatch, a Pole (d. 1783).

III. *Fish.*

You say to the partner at your right: "Do you enjoy fish?"

She (he) replies: "I simply adore fish."

This leads to a discussion of: Fish—
Then, and Now.

Helpful Facts:

1. Fish make notoriously bad pets, whereas seals can be taught to do many novel tricks.
2. Gloucester (Mass.) smells badly in summer.
3. Gloucester (Mass.) smells badly in winter.

IV. *Meat.*

You say to the partner at your right: "Have you ever been through the Stock-Yards?"

She (he) replies: "No." ("Yes.")

This leads to a discussion of: "The Meat Industry in America."

Helpful Facts:

1. Every time a street car goes over the Brooklyn Bridge, a steer is killed in Chicago—and oftener.
2. Raw beefsteak in quantities is harmful to children under two years of age.

[219]

3. A man died recently in Topeka, Kansas, weighing 312 pounds.
4. Many prominent people live on the North Side of Chicago.

V. *Salad.*

You say to the partner at your right: "What is your favorite salad?"
She (he) replies: "I don't know, what's yours?"
This leads to a discussion of: Favorite Things.
Helpful Facts:

1. Richard Barthelmess is married.
2. B. V. D. stands for "Best Value Delivered."
3. Amy Lowell is fond of cigars.

VI. *Dessert.*

You say to the partner at your right: "I love ice cream."
She (he) replies: "So do I."
This leads to a discussion of: Love.
Helpful Facts:

[220]

The Etiquette of Dinners and Balls

1. New York is the hardest state in which to get a divorce in America.
2. Dr. Sigmund Freud is now living in Vienna, Austria.
3. D. H. Lawrence has a black beard.

BALLS AND DANCES

IN order to succeed in the modern ballroom, and especially in the ballrooms of our exclusive country clubs, a young gentleman or lady of fashion must today be possessed of the following two requisites: 1. A "Line." 2. A closed car. The latter of these "sine qua nons" is now owned as a matter of course by most families and is no longer regarded as a mark of distinction. The former requisite, however, is not so common, but it is nevertheless true that any young person with ambition and a good memory can eventually acquire a quite effective "Line." It is a great aid in this direction if one happens to have spent a year or more at one of our leading eastern universities or "finishing schools." These vary, of course, in degree of excellence, but it does not pay to be dogmatic on this subject, and to those who would insist that the Princeton "Line" is more effective than the Harvard ditto, or that the Westover "Line" flows more smoothly than that of Farmington or Spence, one can only say "De gustibus non disputandum est."

"Lines" vary also in accordance with the different types of girls who happen to be using them, and (to misquote a rather vulgar proverb) "What is one girl's food may be another girl's poison." Thus it happens that the "Line" which is most universally and interminably employed by the "beautiful" type of girl (consisting, in its entirety, of the three words "How perfectly priceless") would never in the world do for the young miss whose chief asset is a kind heart or a love for really good books.

MIXED DANCING

A NOTHER quality which is often helpful on the dance floor, especially to girls, is the ability to dance. This seems to have be-

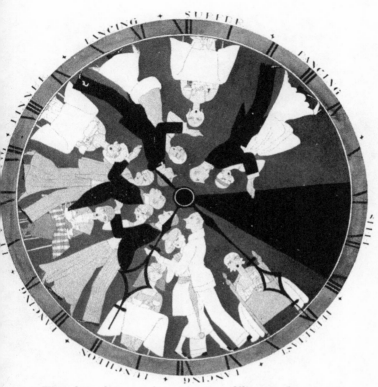

The above diagram (one of many filling the instruc-
tive and refined pages of PERFECT BEHAVIOR)
will serve as a model to any debutante or dancing
man who seriously sets out to achieve social emi-
nence. It is only fair to warn aspirants that rigid
adherence to the formula is essential and that any
slight slackening of the pace is likely to prove fatal.
On the other hand, we confidently guarantee complete success to those who, in reverence and faith,
keep the final goal always in sight. His (or hers)
be it to keep the sacred flame burning and to pass
the torch along from father to son, from mother to
daughter till the end of time, or so long as they do
not make any mesalliances, which is just as
important in America, whatever may be said to
the contrary, as among our "English cousins."

come largely a trick of keeping abreast of the latest "mode" and while, personally, I greatly regret the passing of the stately lancers and other dignified "round dances," yet, if "mixed dancing" has come to stay, it is the duty of every young person to learn to dance as well as possible in the generally accepted manner, even though this often involves some compromising of one's *amour propre.*

But in addition to all these necessary qualifications the really great person—the true super man or woman of the ballroom—must be possessed of that certain divine something, that *je ne sais quoi* ability to rise superior to all occasions, to overcome the most difficult situations, which has distinguished the great men and women of all ages. Joan of Arc had it, George Washington had it, Napoleon had it—and I venture to say that any of these three, had they lived today, would have been a social success. But perhaps this fact can best be illustrated by taking a typical instance in the ballroom in which "When duty whispered low 'Thou must,' the youth replied 'I can.' "

HINTS FOR STAGS

LET us suppose, for example, that you are a young man who has been invited to a dance to be given at the East Shore Country Club. It is your original intention, let us say, to attend as a "stag," but on the afternoon of the party you receive a note from a young lady of your acquaintance asking if you would be so kind as to accompany to the ball a guest of hers, a "sweet girl from South Orange" who was in her class at college.

The correct costume for a dance of this sort is usually a dinner coat with a black or white vest, and when you have robed yourself correctly, you should drive in your car to the young lady's home. There you are presented to the sweet girl from South Orange, who is six feet tall and has protruding teeth. After the customary words of greeting and a few brief bits of pleasantry, you set off with your partner for the dance.

The Etiquette of Dinners and Balls

Arrived at the East Shore Club, you find the party in "full swing," and after shaking hands with your host and hostess, you should ask your partner if she would care to dance.

The first three times that she steps on your left foot, you should politely murmur, "My fault." But when she begins to sing in your ear it is proper to steer her over toward the "stag line" in order to petition for an injunction or a temporary restraining order.

The "stag line" consists of a group of the wisest, shrewdest and most hard-hearted young men ever gathered together under one roof. The original purpose of a "stag line" was to provide a place where unattached young men might stand while searching for a partner, but the institution has now come to be a form of Supreme Court, passing life or death sentence upon the various débutantes who pass before it.

After you have piloted your partner five times along the length of this line you have a pretty fair idea as to her merits or demerits, and, in this particular case, you have a pretty fair idea as to just what the evening holds out for you. When the music stops you should therefore lead the girl over to a chair and ask to be allowed to bring her a glass of punch.

Instead of going directly to the punch bowl, you should turn your steps toward the "stag line." There you will find several young men whom only as late as that afternoon you counted among your very best friends, but who do not, at the present, seem to remember ever having met you before. Seizing the arm of one of these you say, "Tom, I want you to meet——" That is as far as you will get, for Tom will suddenly interrupt you by remarking, "Excuse me a minute, Ed—, I see a girl over there I've simply got to speak to. I'll come right back."

He will not come right back. He will not come back at all. And after you have met with the same response from four other so-called friends, you should return to the South Orange visitor and "carry on."

At the end of the second hour, however, your mind should begin to clear, and if you are at all possessed of the qualifications for future ballroom leadership, you should gradually throw off the slough of despond and determine to make a fight for life, liberty and the pursuit of happiness. And when the music has once more ceased, you should ask your partner if she would not care to take a jaunt in the open air.

"I know a lovely walk," you should say, "across a quaint old bridge."

The rest is, of course, easy. Arrived in the middle of the quaint old bridge, which leads across a cavern some three hundred feet deep, you should quickly seize the tall college graduate, and push her, not too roughly or ungentlemanly, off the bridge.

And, if you are really a genius, and not merely "one of the crowd" you will return to the ballroom and, going up to the young lady who was responsible for your having met the sweet girl from South Orange, you will offer her your arm, and smile invitingly.

"I know a lovely walk," you will say, "across a quaint old bridge."

CPSIA information can be obtained
at www.ICGtesting.com
Printed in the USA
BVHW081916240622
640352BV00003B/3